THE
FIRST
BILLION
IS THE HARDEST

THE FIRST
BILLION
IS THE HARDEST

REFLECTIONS ON A LIFE OF COMEBACKS

AND AMERICA'S ENERGY FUTURE

T. BOONE PICKENS

CROWN
BUSINESS
NEW YORK

Published in the United States by Crown Business,
an imprint of the Crown Publishing Group,
a division of Random House, Inc., New York.
www.crownpublishing.com

Crown Business is a trademark and the Rising Sun colophon is a
registered trademark of Random House, Inc.

Library of Congress Cataloging-in-Publication Data
Pickens, T. Boone (Thomas Boone)
The first billion is the hardest : reflections on a life of comebacks
and America's energy future / T. Boone Pickens.—1st ed.
    p.   cm.
1. Pickens, T. Boone (Thomas Boone)   2. Petroleum industry and
trade—United States.   3. Success in business.   I. Title.
HD9570.P53A3   2008
338.7'622338092—dc22
    [B]   2008010661

978-0-307-39577-1

Printed in the United States of America

Design by Leonard W. Henderson

10 9 8 7 6

First Edition

To my father, Tom Pickens,
a courageous man who saved my life;
my mother, Grace Molonson Pickens,
who gave me life and love;
and my grandmother Nellie Molonson, who taught
me lessons I've used all my life

Contents

There is no limit to what a man can do or where he can go, if he doesn't mind who gets the credit.

—Ronald Reagan

THE

FIRST

BILLION

IS THE HARDEST

Introduction

THERE'S NOTHING BETTER than being the underdog. The more people count me out, the more I count myself in. I don't like to show all my cards too early, and that gives me two distinct advantages: my opponents often get the wrong read on me, and I push myself longer and harder. When it looks like you should pack it in but you still dig in anyway, you also pick up a lot of support. Everybody loves an underdog. Look at Seabiscuit. Throughout my career, being the guy who *isn't* favored to win has earned me a devoted following, a loyal core of supporters that ranges from shareholder activists to people who admire my grit. It's also spurred me to exceed everyone's expectations—on the athletic field, in the oil business, and in taking on Wall Street. Yet in 1996, when I faced my toughest challenges ever, my "dauber was down," as the saying goes. I just wasn't carrying around that self-belief that usually has me doubling my focus when things look grim.

I'd departed Mesa Petroleum, the company I'd founded and led through four decades. My marriage was ending in divorce. My assets seemed to be dwindling daily. And no one was more surprised than I when a doctor diagnosed me as clinically depressed. At sixty-eight, I was well past the official age of retirement, and financially I was at a point where most people would be happy to call it quits. Not this cowboy, though. I had a clear goal for my new company, BP Capital: to become a leading commodities fund.

Let me fast-forward a decade. Last year *Forbes* pegged my net worth at $3 billion. My new bride has captivated me. And my health has never been better. Together, these have been my greatest comebacks. And believe me, my life has not lacked for comebacks.

I hope that with this book I can inspire the millions of Americans who, like me, are entering the fourth quarter. Specifically, I want them to know what I've learned at eighty: the best part of the game truly lies ahead. I'm playing this last period as hard as a walk-on freshman who's just gotten into his first game. I'm also having more fun than I've ever had. I've entered a period of life where I not only value the importance of work but also have a renewed appreciation for my family and endeavor to build the best relationships I possibly can. The time I spend with my children and my grandchildren I enjoy more than ever.

Besides inspiring others who've been counted out *for whatever reason,* what else do I hope to accomplish with this book? Three things. First, I want to reveal the managerial and team-building techniques that have enabled me—especially recently—to enjoy an unprecedented level of success. Second, I want to demonstrate that money can be overrated, but it can also be a precious gift when used unselfishly. If you're interested in hearing how one grateful Texan managed to give $700 million to the causes he loves, stick around. Third, and perhaps most important, I plan to dispel some of the many myths about the oil and gas industry. I've been in this business for over half a century, and I've heard more than my share of stupid ideas. These are the worst:

Myth No. 1: Drilling in the Arctic National Wildlife Refuge will make us energy independent.

Myth No. 2: Ethanol will save the day.

Myth No. 3: Big Oil is manipulating the price of gas at the pumps.

Myth No. 4: The lack of new refineries in the United States is a main contributor to high gasoline prices.

Myth No. 5: New technology will enable us to discover enormous untapped reservoirs of oil.

All these fallacies do is perpetuate misinformation and prevent us from developing an effective national energy plan. Our country is facing a crisis. I fear we have some very dark days ahead, and we must do something about it. I love this country too much to remain silent about the way America's political leadership has failed to tackle what I believe is one of the greatest threats ever to face this nation: our crippling dependence on foreign oil.

In the final chapters of this book, I spell out what I'm convinced is America's increasingly dangerous addiction to imported oil and the economic perils that lie ahead if we don't act fast, particularly with respect to certain alternative technologies. Action, that's what's important. In this book, I don't just identify the problem; I offer answers. Our biggest problem is leadership. For decades, we've lacked the leadership at the federal level to address our growing dependence on foreign oil. We've all heard the empty promises and seen the results of shallow policies.

"Elect me president, and America will become energy independent!" Every candidate says it, and once they're elected not one does a thing about it. The cost of our failure to secure this vital lifeline is staggering. By importing foreign oil to meet our ever-increasing demands, the United States is transferring close to

$1 trillion a year (assuming a price of $150 per barrel) to foreign nations that, with few exceptions, don't really like us. It's the greatest transfer of wealth in human history, and it has to be stopped *now*. We need a plan to radically reduce our dependence on foreign oil, and we need leadership able to carry it out. Otherwise, we risk losing our status as a superpower.

I'll outline my national energy plan here. Is it perfect? No. Is it a realistic start? You bet, and it's time to get serious and begin working on it. I believe our oil addiction is the greatest threat facing America in the twenty-first century. I also believe that, as with all crises our country has faced, determination and ingenuity can yield the solutions we seek. I hope you enjoy this book and take to heart its most important messages. Most crucially, I hope you get involved in the campaign to address the crisis of foreign oil imports.

I've spent more than a year working on this book, and my goal was not just to create an interesting read. It was to issue a wake-up call to every American who cares as much about this country as I do.

T. Boone Pickens
Dallas, Texas
May 22, 2008

CHAPTER 1

Blood, Guts, and Feathers

Booneism #1: Don't rush the monkey, and you'll see a better show.

RISK HAS ALWAYS BEEN a part of my life. I'm not sure whether I'm drawn to it or it's drawn to me, but at every point in my eighty years, I've been faced with a challenge, and in just about every instance I've taken it. Even my birth was a do-or-die proposition.

My mother went into labor on May 21, 1928. It was a long ordeal, and things weren't going well. The doctor, George Wallace, took my father, Tom, into a small room and closed the door. He had a grave look on his face, and my father immediately spotted a large book on a table. He assumed it was a Bible.

"Your wife has been in labor a long time, and she can't deliver. I'm worried about her. You can save your wife or your baby, but not both," Dr. Wallace said.

My father wasn't an either-or sort of guy. He was a natural-born risk taker and the son of a Methodist preacher. And so when Dr. Wallace, who happened to be a surgeon, told him that it was either my mother, Grace, or me, my father refused to choose. He pleaded with the doctor to try the first Caesarean section in that hospital's history.

"Well, Tom, I've heard about a C-section, but I've never done one," the doctor said. He pointed to the book on the table. "All I've got is a page and a half and one picture in that medical book to go by."

"We're gonna pray, and you're gonna deliver the baby," my father told him.

A short time later, Dr. Wallace came out of the operating room with a broad smile on his face. He had just performed his first Caesarean. The procedure wouldn't be repeated at that hospital for more than twenty-five years. Dr. Wallace was a surgeon—no general practitioner would have ever performed a C-section—and he'd lived in that small town in Oklahoma for just two years. The odds of him being the man that delivered me were slim at best. I've always thought I was the luckiest man alive, and right from the start I proved it.

"You've got a little boy," Dr. Wallace told my father. "And your wife is doing fine."

THE SIGN READ: WELCOME TO HOLDENVILLE. WHERE THE PAVEMENT ENDS, THE WEST BEGINS, AND THE ROCK ISLAND CROSSES THE FRISCO. And that, sports fans, was Holdenville, a railroad town in eastern Oklahoma, a speck in the grand sweep of the Great Plains, where the open land was vast, rolling, and endless.

My father was in the oil business. Outgoing, generous, a great storyteller, and a gifted poker player, he arrived in Holdenville at age twenty-five. He was a lawyer but soon realized that law was nowhere near as exciting as oil. So he became an independent land man, convincing landowners to lease him their mineral rights, which he in turn sold to oil companies. I was an only child, but I was always surrounded by family who lived next door: my grand-mother Nellie Molonson; my widowed aunt, Ethel Reed; and my cousin Billy Bob, who was like an older brother to me. My parents were hardworking, thrifty, honest, and self-sufficient. They came from an era when a job was viewed as a privilege, not a right. I grew up during the Great Depression, but our family always had food on the table. My grandmother had a large vegetable garden, and each night she served fresh or canned vegetables. Some nights we had meat to go with the vegetables, and some nights we didn't, but we were never hungry.

My mother, Grace—the disciplinarian in our family—instilled important lessons in me early on, which prepared me for the challenges ahead. During the war, she ran our area's Office of Price Administration, which rationed gasoline and other goods. She had a great sense of integrity; if she said she would do something, you could consider it done. My grandmother Nellie was so disciplined that most nights she would have only one cup of tea and a slice of dry whole wheat toast for supper. She taught me things I've never forgotten.

"Remember, a fool and his money are soon parted," she said when I told her I was going to spend 50 cents on a haircut, a movie, and a bag of popcorn.

"Sometime, everybody has to learn to sit on their own bottom," she said whenever I asked for too much help with something.

As soon as I was old enough, I started mowing lawns, which I did until I could take on a paper route at age twelve. I began on a street grandly named Broadway of America with the smallest route in town: twenty-eight houses with a penny-a-paper profit per day. When other routes came open next to mine, I talked my supervisor into letting me take them on. Within five years my route grew from 28 papers to 156 and I had saved close to $200, which I hid in a hole under the floor in my closet. It was my first experience in the takeover field: expansion by acquisition.

In my first year as a paperboy, I found a wallet on the sidewalk. Inside it were the name and address of the owner. I delivered it to the man, and he gave me a dollar reward. It was a windfall. My mother, grandmother, and aunt were on the porch when I got home. They didn't respond as I'd expected or hoped to the news of my finding the wallet and getting the reward. They didn't look at one another. They didn't have to. They were so much alike that their heads moved in unison, almost as if each head was attached to the others by a string. I pleaded my case over and over, but they sent me straight back to return the dollar to the man.

"You are not going to be paid to be honest," my grandmother told me.

So I had to go back to the man and give his dollar back.

"No, no, this is for you!"

"I know!"

"And you should have it!"

"I know!"

But I also knew better than to go against anything my mother, grandmother, and aunt told me. I gave the money back and headed home on my bike in a downpour. I damn near drowned. I got home drenched and looking for sympathy. I could play the pitiful routine really well. Aunt Ethel didn't buy it.

"If you hadn't argued with us, you'd have been back before it rained," she said.

In 1927 a major oil field had been discovered in Seminole, a sleepy little town just down the road from Holdenville. It had turned into a boomtown. By 1938 the search for big oil in our area had run its course. My father began to run out of luck. Instead of playing it safe with land deals, he started investing in wildcats, which were wells drilled by independent oilmen in uncharted territory. Successful wildcats came with big payoffs—but at great risk. Our family was soon pinched. The yellow Pierce Arrow sedan my father had bought for my mother during a streak of good luck was gone; our Chevy wasn't new anymore. Dad took a job with a regular paycheck at Phillips Petroleum Company. In 1943, he was reassigned to an office in the Texas Panhandle. My mother and I joined him in 1944. I was sixteen, loved Holdenville, and didn't want to leave. But move we did. I learned important lessons from my high school basketball coach in Amarillo, T. G. Hull. He told us to play all out but not to dwell on either successes or losses. He taught me that when the game is over, it's over.

Our team did well in high school basketball, and I attended Texas A&M on a basketball scholarship. A little short and slow for college basketball, I lost my scholarship after a year and transferred to Oklahoma A&M at Stillwater (now Oklahoma State University) my sophomore year. At my father's urging, I decided to switch my major to geology. When I graduated at the age of twenty-two, Phillips Petroleum hired me as a geologist. It was a difficult time in the oil industry. Geologist jobs were in short supply. By this time in my life, I had mowed lawns and thrown papers. I'd worked on a drilling rig as a roughneck, on the railroad as a fireman, and in a refinery. Hard work was nothing new to me. "What kind of master plan did you have back in your early career?" people ask me. I was married and had a child when I took my job with Phillips; the master plan was simply to get everybody fed.

Back when I was with Phillips, I was working with three geologists and a couple of engineers on a joint interest well. I was making

$5,000 a year. One of the geologists asked, "If you could lock in a salary right now for the rest of your life and work until you're sixty-five years old, what would you sign up for?" Everybody thought about it; I was the only one who answered. I had a wife and two kids by then and wanted to ensure that my family lived comfortably.

What would I work for without raises until I turned sixty-five?

"Twenty-five thousand dollars," I said finally. At that period of my life, security was very important to me. Thank goodness it was only a conversation.

AT PHILLIPS, I met the monster: Big Oil. Phillips was one of the twenty largest corporations in America. It had twenty thousand employees, chemical and plastic divisions, refineries, an international operation, hundreds of Phillips 66 gas stations, and two dozen exploration and production offices—all run by a big and sluggish army of bureaucrats. I went to work in the home office in Bartlesville, Oklahoma. Every morning a bell rang at five minutes before eight, signaling you to your desk, just like in school. At noon, everyone would be standing by the door, waiting for the lunch bell. At one, the bell would ring, signaling that lunch was over. The final bell rang at five, and they didn't want anybody staying past quitting time. (I once got reprimanded for staying until six.) Paranoia was rampant. What sickened me most was the waste. Management was incapable of listening to or even considering alternative ideas to save the company money or find more oil.

"If you're unhappy, why don't you quit?" my wife asked me after one of many nights of hearing my complaints. I don't think she meant it or dreamed that I would actually do it. After three years, five months, twenty-one days, and four hours, I did exactly what she suggested. I went over the wall.

"I want your car keys and your credit card," the division manager told me.

I walked out of the office with all of my belongings in a pasteboard box and headed for the bus. Although I was more than a little scared, I felt as though somebody had taken his foot off my neck. We had two young daughters by then and another baby on the way. Christmas was just around the corner.

My wife was surprised when I walked into the house.

"What are you doing home at three o'clock?" she asked.

"I just quit," I said.

"Have you lost your mind?"

"No, I did what you told me to do last night," I said. "You told me to quit if I didn't like where I worked, so I did."

"I didn't mean that! I didn't think you would actually do it."

She paused for a minute.

"Boone, what are you going to do now?"

Someday I would challenge Big Oil, but right then I had more pressing needs. I had to make a living. I was twenty-six when I went out on my own in 1954, the youngest independent geologist in the Texas Panhandle. I used the $1,300 in my Phillips thrift plan as a down payment on a 1955 Ford station wagon and started out as a consultant doing well-site work for $75 a day. Those days were too few. My back was against the wall. When I was doing well-site work, I often slept in my car and shaved in service stations. At the end of my first year on my own I had put together seven drilling deals in addition to my consulting work. I knew I was not going to get rich on $75 a day. But if I could put enough deals together, I could make a decent living and accumulate some equity. Maybe then I could get rich.

Two years later I formed my first oil company with two

investors. They put in $1,250 each for half the stock and estab-
lished a $100,000 line of credit for our new company. I gave them
a $2,500 note for my half. The company was called Petroleum
Exploration Inc. (PEI). Then I hit the road again to find more
investors willing to finance a drilling program for a group of wells.
Except for a few members of my family, no one gave me a prayer
of succeeding. My single-minded focus gave me an edge: I was now
going to succeed or fall on my ass. In fact I always think I have an
edge, but I love to be the underdog.

One day a geologist friend said, "You're getting pretty unpopu-
lar with the other geologists here in town. You never come over to
the Embers and have a drink after work." The Embers was a bar
three or four blocks away from my office.

"Well, you guys are going over there at three o'clock in the afternoon. That's not after work," I told him.

He didn't think that was funny. We were in a pretty rough period
in the industry, and all of us were struggling. "We're all having a
hard time," he said.

"Yeah, it's a tough time for the industry, but I don't think the
Embers at three o'clock in the afternoon is the place to solve anything," I said.

"Look, Boone, why don't you come by and have a drink with us
anyway?"

"OK," I said, and stopped off at the Embers after work. By then,
they had already had three or four beers, so everybody was getting
pretty loose. The Embers had some attractive waitresses, and they
were all laughing and cutting up. I had a beer and hung around for
a little while.

"I'm heading home," I said. "You guys hang around here and
somebody's going to get into trouble."

I wasn't trying to be self-righteous, but a couple of years later, three of the five guys there told me that my comments had had an impact on them. Stay away from the temptation. Temptation scares me to death. Just don't go where you are going to get exposed. I'd break down just as quick as another guy, but I just didn't—and still don't—give myself the opportunity. Again, it's simple. There is work, and there is home, and there aren't any stops in between. Now, you may ask, "Gosh, Boone, are you so rigid that's all you ever did?" No. I played golf and I hunted on the weekends. I've been drunk, but never two nights in a row. I was a normal, red-blooded American guy. Only I decided early on to concentrate on business and home and to omit the distractions and temptations that mess up so many lives.

In 1962 I got PEI a very low-risk prospect in the Panhandle. We had a good run and drilled ninety-eight straight oil wells in Hutchinson County. By now our small company had grown to twenty-three employees and three hundred investors. Despite the fact that I had no management experience or executive training, I was starting to gain confidence in my ability to run a company. In 1964 we went public and changed the name from PEI to Mesa Petroleum. The name came from the tabletop mesas that rise from the plains of the Texas Panhandle. On April 30, we had 239 investors-turned-stockholders and issued 420,052 shares of stock. We were debt-free and a public company. We made a $435,310 profit on revenue of $1.5 million our first year. I thought it was a very good start.

By 1968, revenue had grown to $6.2 million, with profits of $1.4 million. We had 62 billion cubic feet of natural gas reserves and a couple of million barrels of oil at a time when oil prices were stagnant and the industry was depressed. I was impatient with our progress, but we were doing pretty well. I felt we needed to grow faster. This could be done either by making a big discovery or by acquisitions. We didn't have the prospects to make a big discovery, so I began looking at possible companies to acquire. In early 1968, I found a good prospect, a diamond in the rough: the Hugoton Production Company of Garden City, Kansas. Their largest stockholder was Clark Estates, a New York money management firm that owned 11 percent. Not very impressive, but they controlled the company. Hugoton owned a substantial part of the Hugoton Field, the largest natural gas field in the United States. Based on reserves, Hugoton was fifteen times bigger than we were. But Hugoton had a no-growth structure and wasn't set up to get the best price for its gas. We were. It was a perfect match.

I went to New York with Wales Madden, one of our directors, to meet Hugoton's president, Mike Nicolais. Over dinner Nicolais said that he had backed away from three previous mergers, but he added that he would still consider one under the right circumstances. I invited him to Texas, and he accepted. I gave him a tour of Mesa's operation and showed him how much we had grown in just a short time. Even though Nicolais mentioned that at forty I was young to be running such a big operation, I thought he was impressed. We had a high level of energy and an impressive track record. Hugoton had huge reserves and a solid operation but little vision for the future.

When I dropped Nicolais at the airport, I told him, "I hope we convinced you that Mesa and Hugoton would be a good fit." He gave me some assurance but cautioned me that he still had to sell any merger to his board. A week later he called and politely declined, saying they had no interest in a merger with Mesa. Back at the office, I slumped in my chair, considering our options. The match was just too perfect. *If only...*

By late afternoon, it hit me—one of those life-changing moments. It came to me in the shower. I made up my mind that I was going to try a takeover, one that would set us up for even bigger and bolder moves down the road. Taking no for an answer would not be an option. We were going after Hugoton.

I was about to learn an invaluable lesson about the power of bold moves and big deals. Dow Hamm, who was executive vice president of Arco, told me something I'll never forget.

"Boone, you will spend just as much time on a big deal as on a little deal. In big deals, there's always serendipity. You'll find a lot of *lagniappe*." That's a term folks in my part of the country use for a bonus or fringe benefit. "There's so much in a big deal that nobody can evaluate," Dow told me. "Once you get in there you'll find out what I'm talking about. The bigger, the better." I am sure that was what happened when Bob Anderson at Arco acquired Sinclair.

Hugoton was my first run at a company, and twenty years after we made the deal we were still finding plenty of lagniappe. Of course, it took a huge effort to make the deal. Acquisitions were fairly common in the late 1960s, but most were friendly deals. My partner, Lawton Clark; Wales Madden; and I worked closely together in those days. We felt like the Wright Brothers when they took off in the first airplane: *Would this thing fly?*

We took a small position in Hugoton's stock for $1.3 million. We didn't have the money to buy more, so we did the next best thing: made an unsolicited offer of Mesa securities for Hugoton stock, one share of a newly created Mesa preferred stock for each share of Hugoton common stock. It was an unusual offer, but one that showed the street we were serious. In a few weeks our activities upgraded the market value of Hugoton from $77 million to $137 million, an all-time high.

We had mustered enough money to bring our ownership stake to 17 percent. It was enough to make us the company's biggest shareholder, and management was starting to take us seriously. On October 23 the company tried to do an end run by announcing a merger with Los Angeles–based Reserve Oil and Gas Company. What a dog. The company was a loser. It was a lucky break for us. Reserve's earnings were only 34 cents a share, compared with our $1.83, and we were finding substantially more oil and gas. Hugoton needed to get a two-thirds vote to do the merger with Reserve; to block the deal, we needed another 17 percent. We couldn't afford to buy any more stock, so we began lobbying shareholders to vote against the merger or at least not vote for it. That strategy worked. We weren't even close to having enough stock to take over the company, but we were going to block Hugoton's merger with Reserve. Hoping to break the stalemate, Mike Nicolais agreed to let me come to New York for a meeting of the Hugoton board.

Everyone was against me. They asked hostile questions, which I answered calmly. Wales Madden had told me before the meeting started, "Pick, stay cool." One of the company's directors, John E. Bierwirth, head of National Distillers, rose from his seat. "I'm leaving," he said. "I'm not going to waste any more of my time listening to this guy."

I seized the moment. "Mr. Bierwirth, how much stock in Hugoton do you own?" I asked.

"The National Distillers' employee pension plan owns ten thousand shares," he shot back.

"I didn't ask you about the employee pension plan. What do you own personally?" I asked.

That lit a fuse within him; his face turned beet red. He didn't say anything.

"Let me help you. Hugoton's proxy material shows that you own one hundred shares."

He looked like he was so mad he could have bitten himself. He just glared at me.

"I own seven thousand shares personally, and Mesa owns 17 percent of Hugoton," I said. "It looks like I've got a lot more confidence in Hugoton than you do."

It couldn't have been planned any better. Bierwirth was so tight he wouldn't have paid a dime to watch a pissant eat a bale of hay. I had proven that not only to him but to the entire Hugoton board. He got up, slammed his chair against the table, and stormed out of the room. Wales Madden and I were then excused from the meeting. I was making enemies, but I was scoring some points, too.

"You know, not everyone here dislikes you, Mr. Pickens," a receptionist told me just outside the door. I smiled. "You may not realize this, but some of the directors are on your side." That was something I desperately needed to hear.

We increased our stake to 28 percent with our exchange offer. It would be a stretch, but we could now borrow enough to bring our ownership up to the 34 percent level. We didn't have to go that far. Hugoton knew we were there to stay. By early January 1969, Mike Nicolais surrendered over the phone: "Come to New York, we're ready to talk terms."

On April 7, 1969, the shareholders voted to combine the companies. Hugoton Production Company and Mesa Petroleum merged, and Mesa was the survivor. It would prove to be one of the most important deals I would ever make. Mesa now had the reserves and the balance sheet to play in the big league and compete for acreage anywhere, including federal offshore leases in the Gulf of Mexico.

In 1970, soon after the Hugoton deal, we acquired Pubco

Petroleum, which gave us divisions in the Rocky Mountains and Permian Basin. Between 1968 and 1972, Mesa grew rapidly from a profitable small oil and gas company into a serious player with $92 million in revenues, $15 million in profits, and $189 million in assets. All of this after only eight years as a public company.

Our tempo was picking up. We were on our way.

> ***Booneism #2:*** *Chief executives who themselves own few shares of their companies have no more feeling for the stockholders than they do for baboons in Africa.*

TODAY MERGERS AND acquisitions are commonplace, shareholder value is a hallmark of well-run companies, and chief executives are scrutinized by their shareholders, the media, and the SEC. And I have gotten a lot of credit for changing the way companies are run. It was another world back then. There was a time in the 1980s when excessive perks by executives went largely unreported. These executives ran their companies like private fiefdoms, all at the shareholders' expense. You may have forgotten what was going on during this period. But I was intensely involved in the big changes that were taking place in corporate America.

Before I focus on the present and the future, it's important to flash back to the past. The oil booms in the 1920s and 1930s were the result of the discovery of great oil fields. Fifty years later, most of the big fields had been found. Another boom began, which was more the result of price increases than the discovery of new fields. It resulted in a drilling frenzy that lasted a decade. We were getting our first glimpse of the oil industry of the future. The catalyst was the Arab oil embargo of 1973, when members of the Organization of the Petroleum Exporting Countries (OPEC) agreed to production quotas and a handful of small countries halfway around the world disrupted the most powerful nation on earth. By 1979, gasoline shortages forced Americans to wait in line at gas stations, the cost of home heating oil soared, and Washington urged citizens to keep thermostats at 68 degrees in winter. This was just a preview of what was to come thirty years later, but OPEC was just learning at this point.

There was no worldwide shortage of oil; OPEC was simply withholding it from the market. The situation reached crisis level when the shah of Iran was deposed and Iranian production nosedived. It drove the world oil price from $13 to $30 a barrel practically overnight. By December 1981 oil topped $40 a barrel. Newly discovered natural gas was soaring at more than $10 Mcf (thousand cubic feet). As a result, the U.S. economy went into recession in all quarters except the oil industry, where a boom of epic proportions was raging.

While Americans waited in lines for gasoline, oil companies were up to their armpits in cash. Profits doubled and tripled in the space of a year. Even though the companies were producing less oil, the higher prices led to record profits, and some of the firms deluded themselves into thinking that the profits were due to their leadership instead of increases caused by OPEC. I've said that giving the good old boys of Big Oil excess cash flow is like handing a rabbit a head of lettuce for safekeeping. They made some of the worst deals in the history of corporate America during this period. For example, Mobil paid $1.86 billion for Montgomery Ward as part of its plan for diversification. It was a disaster. When a 1984 issue of *Fortune* focused on the seven worst mergers of the decade, four of them involved big oil companies.

Money management was something I learned early on. Waste was a big deal in our family. My grandmother saw to that. She was a frugal woman. The first time I ever heard the word *inventory* was from her when I was a kid.

"Why would anybody buy two tubes of Ipana toothpaste?" she asked me. And as soon as she said that, I knew there was a lesson coming.

"Sonny, always buy one tube, and when you know you are running out you can roll it up and get another week out of it easy. Why should we carry inventory for Charlie Amos?" she asked.

Charlie Amos owned a drugstore in Holdenville, and my grandmother's lesson on inventory control stuck with me for a lifetime. I don't buy toothpaste or any other items in bunches. I buy nice clothes, but I don't let them stack up. I shop for clothing once a year.

I hang on to stuff. Some of my possessions I bought long ago. I carry a bird-shaped silver pillbox purchased in 1959. I've handled it so much the engraving has worn off. There's the $750 Rolex I bought in Vienna in 1964, which cost me so much that I had to max out two credit cards: mine and one that belonged to my friend Wales Madden. I also have a pair of infinitely resoled penny loafers from 1957. I almost lost them on a freeway in Riverside, California. We were in our station wagon, I had my kids, and it was crowded. Our clothes were in a luggage carrier on the top of the car, and I had left it unzipped. We were going down the freeway, and I looked in the rearview mirror and saw clothes blowing all over the freeway. I pulled over to the shoulder and backed up slowly. There was a lot of traffic, and the clothes had scattered on the other side of the road.

"I'm going to time it so I can run across and get the clothes when there's a gap in the traffic," I told my wife. "I think I can get everything in two trips." My son got on the floor of the station wagon because he thought I was going to get hit. I ran out and picked up our clothes, including the loafers, and ran back. I've had those shoes ever since, and I still wear them occasionally. I somehow think they're lucky. And when things are not going so good I wear them.

When I leave a room today I turn off the lights, remembering what my grandmother told me: "Sonny, next month I'm going to send you the electric bill and let you see how much these lights cost." It was my first exposure to a lesson that has guided my career: Always think like an owner.

I have been frugal in my businesses, always keeping in mind that shareholders are the owners of a company, while members of management are employees. When I was in my thirties, I was invited on a two-day fishing trip on Yellowstone Lake with a group of executives from major oil companies, large independents, and service companies. I was the youngest in the group. The trip was memorable because it was when I first met Jimmy Lee, then the number-two man at Gulf Oil, but soon to be number one. He was a nice guy and that was about it. He also wasn't much of a card player, and that was about it too.

On that trip and other gatherings with the leaders in the oil industry, I picked up some disturbing signals. The top executives seemed to have one thing in common. Most had spent their entire working lives in one organization. They were bureaucrats and caretakers who had moved up by avoiding the one thing that to my mind is the difference between success and failure: taking risks. They also didn't seem interested in opinions other than their own.

> ***Booneism #3:*** *Far too many executives are more con-*
> *cerned with the four Ps—pay, perks, power, and prestige—*
> *than with making profits for shareholders.*

THE ARROGANCE OF some CEOs was unbelievable. One story I like to tell involved a man whose family founded Union Oil Company of California, which later become Unocal. He was the company's largest individual shareholder and a director. At a director's meeting, he proposed an increase in the dividend. Fred Hartley, the CEO, responded with typical managerial disdain for shareholders:"Have you lost your goddamned mind? Why would we give people we don't know a bunch of money?" That was the attitude toward shareholders in corporate America at that time.

Even though Mesa grew explosively between 1973 and 1981, I was not comfortable. If OPEC opened the valves, prices would fall through the floor. I remember giving a speech and telling the audience,"I can see who controls the oil. I don't know them, and we don't speak the same language. If they decide to open up and produce, we're looking at ten-dollar oil very quick."

We had put a lot of money into our Canadian operations. By 1979, the country was making some serious political changes, and they concerned me. We sold off Mesa's lucrative properties there in a seller's market for $600 million. It was a pretty good return, considering that we had gone to Canada in 1959 with just $35,000. Canada had been good to us, but we were now starting to focus almost exclusively on the United States.

Production for most large oil companies was in a state of decline; they were producing more oil than they were finding. Independents like Mesa were doing better. We had increased our reserves for eighteen straight years, but this was getting increasingly hard to do. I was intent on growth, but there were fewer and fewer opportunities. My calculations showed that by 1985 we would need an annual exploration and development budget of $1 billion to replace reserves. We were stretching the balance sheet beyond where I wanted to take it. Then, in a speech to Merrill Lynch money managers in New York, I mentioned the words that the oil industry still doesn't want to hear: reserve replacement.

"Mesa is not going to hang around with a depleting reserve base," I told them. "If we fail to replace our reserves for two years in a row, I'll consider that a trend and we'll figure out something else to do or we'll get out of the business." In bed a few nights later, I had a thought.

You can solve your problem by making Mesa smaller: spin off some of the company's reserves to shareholders. We would create a royalty trust that would represent 90 percent ownership in some of Mesa's oil and gas properties, and the cash flow from production would be distributed to the shareholders. Thus, our reserve base— the oil and gas properties that Mesa retained—would be smaller, making replacement of reserves easier. When Mesa Royalty Trust was announced in June 1979, our stock price was $54. When the trust was approved by shareholders that October, the price was $86. It was obvious that management was doing a good job for the owners. It was some time before anyone followed our lead.

CHAPTER 2

"A Big Deal Takes as Much Time as a Little Deal"

Booneism #4: As my father used to say, "There are three reasons we can't do it. First, we don't have the money, and it doesn't make a damn about the other two."

BY THE EARLY 1980s, I had been working on an idea for some time, and it would change everything for Mesa. I figured it was vastly cheaper to look for oil and gas reserves on the floor of the New York Stock Exchange than to explore for them in the Gulf of Mexico or some other untapped frontier. We created a plan to go for broke. We would seek out the most vulnerable, undervalued, poorly managed big oil companies, then target one and make a major investment in that company. We would push the management of that company to do what they should have been doing in the first place: returning value to their stockholders. There was a steep discount in the value of these companies when measured against their underlying assets, in this case, oil and gas. If management dug in and refused, we would mount a takeover attack and either force them to make changes or get control of the company and do it ourselves.

It was a big idea, and initially a tough one to sell. It was a dust-off of the old Hugoton blueprint but on a much larger scale. We were back to acquisitions, but it turned out to be much more than that. In the process we would restructure an industry and even influence corporate America. We had no idea that was going to happen. Back then, nobody dared to challenge the giants. Mesa was a good-sized independent oil company, and it bordered on craziness to even think about going after one of the giants. But remember, Hugoton had been fifteen times our size.

Cities Service — not quite a giant, but close — was our first target. Not long ago, someone asked me at a speech why I went after Cities Service, and I told the audience to listen closely because the punch line of the story would be the answer to his question.

A guy goes into a bar at three in the afternoon with his dog.

"No dogs allowed here," says the bartender.

"But this is a special dog," says the guy. "First, he's a talking dog. Second, he drinks."

Intrigued and without customers in the bar, the bartender replies, "OK, put the dog up on the bar stool and tell me what he drinks."

"A martini, straight up," the guy said. "He'll just lap it."

The bartender served the dog a martini and his owner a Miller Lite. After the dog's owner went to the men's room, the bartender turned to the dog.

"Are you really a talking dog?"

"Yes, I am. My name is George. What's your name?"

"Toby."

After the dog took a couple of laps from the martini, the bartender asked, "Would you do something for me, George?"

"Sure, if I can."

"There's a newsstand on the corner. You don't even have to cross the street. Would you get me the evening newspaper? It's three-fifteen and they sell out at three-thirty, and my wife will kill me if I don't bring the paper home."

"Sure," said George. "Put a dollar bill in my mouth, because it's easier for me to carry than change."

Toby opened the door and George ran off with the buck in his mouth.

The owner came back from the men's room and asked, "Where's George?"

Toby told him what he'd done.

"He can take care of that," the owner said. "He'll be back in a minute."

After about fifteen minutes, when George hadn't returned, the owner decided to check on him. He stepped out of the bar and saw George up on this poodle.

"George! I've never known you to do anything like this!"

"Hell," said George, "this is the first time I've had money."

That's the reason we went after Cities Service. It was the first time we had real money.

Based in Tulsa, Cities Service ranked thirty-eighth on the Fortune 500 list and was the nineteenth-largest oil company in America.

Mesa had been a stockholder in Cities Service for several years, to keep watch on the company and because it was so undervalued. Like many other oil companies, Cities Service had been depleting its reserves for a decade. Its stock sold at about one-third of the value of the underlying assets. Cities' CEO, Charles J. Waidelich, had been with the company for thirty-one years but owned very little stock.

For two years I had listened to investment bankers tell us there was no way for Mesa to take over Cities Service. Cities was just too big. However, times had changed, and we decided to quit listening to the bankers. Good decision. Also, we didn't have any other prospect for making money. In early 1981 we came up with our own plan: to seek a partner and launch a takeover.

One of our first stops for potential takeover partners was Gulf Oil. I knew their CEO, Jimmy Lee, from the Yellowstone fishing trip and thought he would be easy to talk to. "We would like to look at anything you think would make sense and make us money," Lee said when I called to see if he would join me in a bid for Cities. He added that his board might even live with a hostile takeover attempt, but he wanted me to bring our plan to him and show him what I was talking about. So we went to Pittsburgh to meet him in February 1981. I gave Lee and his CFO, Harold Hammer, a two-hour presentation. Lee took notes; Hammer didn't. He just sat there looking as if he would rather have been undergoing a root canal. I went through my pitch, showing them our takeover strategy.

Then Lee dropped a bombshell: "Boone, I'm sorry, but we can't be in a hostile deal." It was just the opposite of what he'd told me on the phone the day before. On the way out the door, Mesa's CFO, Gaines Godfrey, said just what I was thinking: "Do you realize what those bastards did? They know exactly what we're going to do."

Next stop: Marathon Oil. We visited their home office in Findlay, Ohio, late one Saturday morning. "You should be running this company," Marathon CEO Harold "Hoop" Hoopman told me. He said he was interested in joining our deal, although he was concerned about what a hostile takeover attempt might do to his company's image. Ten days later he called and said he couldn't do it. It was probably a good thing. Marathon soon found itself under siege by takeover attempts. First, Mobil launched a hostile bid for the company; they eventually lost out to U.S. Steel. We also had a brief meeting with U.S. Steel about the Cities deal. We were educating these guys all over the place. Gulf. Marathon. U.S. Steel. Little did I know that they would use our ideas but not do business with us.

To make an offer of $45 a share for Cities, we needed $2.3 billion. We had to have help. Days before our tender offer was to be launched, Cities struck, announcing a plan to . . . make a tender offer to buy Mesa's stock. This was an odd twist, but it was not something we hadn't talked about.

The fact that an offer for Mesa was announced gave Cities a real advantage on timing. In a tender offer, the bidder has to wait twenty business days before paying for the stock that has been tendered. In this case, Cities would be able to buy our stock on June 28. Even if we could have begun our offer the next day—which was impossible, since we didn't have our financing set—we wouldn't be able to buy Cities stock until after June 29. They could buy us before we could buy them.

Cities announced its offer on the Friday before Memorial Day. We spent the weekend scrambling. I was taking a shower on Memorial Day when I thought, "Why don't we try a bear hug offer?" A bear hug is a ploy that puts pressure on a target company's directors. It is not a hostile offer. It's made to the company's board rather than to the stockholders, and it's contingent on board approval. At best it was a weak offer. The difference here was that we couldn't just walk away if the Cities board turned us down; we would have to come up with something else fast.

I called Cities CEO Chuck Waidelich in Tulsa and put the bear hug in motion.

"Chuck, our offer for Cities is fifty dollars a share."

"We're not interested, and it's not a formal offer anyway. It's not in writing," snapped Waidelich.

"Hell," I said, "we'll have an offer to you in three hours."

"I don't want it."

"We've got to bring it to you now. The stockholders of both our companies need to know that we've made you an offer. We'll make a public announcement, and I suppose you'll have to call your board of directors."

"I have no intention of calling them," Waidelich insisted. "We're not interested."

It didn't matter. My phone call had accomplished its purpose: an offer was on the table, and we would make it public. We drafted a press release, giving the details of our offer.

Almost immediately, the news was all over the media.

We were almost back in the game. Or at least we thought we were.

Still seeking partners, we flew out to see the Doctor—the legendary Dr. Armand Hammer, CEO of Occidental Petroleum. We arrived in Los Angeles at 1 a.m. Pacific time and went straight to Occidental's offices. We were ushered into the executive conference room, which was filled with people. At the head of the table sat Dr. Hammer, so exhausted that he slept as we made our presentation. I would have, too, if I hadn't been speaking. We had come from Eastern time in New York, so it was 4 a.m. for us. Oxy wasn't ready to move on our idea.

Then Gulf dropped a bomb, announcing a $63 per share cash offer for 100 percent of Cities. Remember, we'd shown the deal to them and given them our game plan. It was a ridiculous offer, and far more than the company was worth. Six weeks later, Gulf announced that it was yanking its bid to buy Cities, whose stock dropped to a low of $30 per share. Then only one week after that, Cities dropped their bomb: they were merging with Dr. Armand Hammer's Occidental Petroleum. Bombs were everywhere, and I guess the Doctor hadn't been sleeping through our presentation after all. Occidental bought Cities for $53 a share in what would be a $4 billion deal. Mesa made a $31.5 million profit on the rise in the price of shares we had accumulated throughout the deal.

We learned a lot in this deal. There were a lot more dumb sons of bitches than I could have ever imagined, and I'm not so sure I wasn't one of them. Even though we hadn't succeeded in taking over Cities, the attempt had proved I was right in my belief that shaking up Big Oil could be profitable. We'd stumbled our way through and picked up pocket change of $31 million. We would do a better job next time, and I was eager for an even bigger opportunity.

Booneism #5: The higher a monkey climbs a tree, the more people can see his ass.

ONE COMPANY STOOD above the rest as the dumbest of them all. Gulf Oil was the nation's sixth-largest oil company and fit our takeover criteria to a tee. Gulf Oil had the most assets, and they were grossly undervalued. It was a real endorsement for their weak management. They had struggled through three decades of

pathetic leadership, and it was time for a change. In 1983, Gulf had
400,000 shareholders, 40,000 employees, $20 billion in assets, and
$30 billion in annual revenues. Based on our analysis, we figured they
were worth $80 to $100 a share. Yet the stock was selling in the high
$30s because of the company's management and reputation. They
were an embarrassment to the industry. While the prospect of Mesa
actually acquiring a giant like Gulf was a stretch, we believed we
could get management working and get the stock price up. This
would benefit all shareholders. We arranged $1.1 billion in credit and
formed the Gulf Investors Group. Mesa owned two-thirds of the
group. By August we were ready to start buying shares of Gulf Oil.

Within two months we had spent $638 million to acquire 9 per-
cent of all outstanding Gulf shares at an average cost of $43 a
share. That made us Gulf's largest shareholder, larger even than the
legendary Mellon family, the founders of the company. We did the
deal with what *Time* magazine later described as "cloak-and-
dagger stealth." We gave the Gulf deal a code name: Barrel Cactus,
after a plant in my office. We drew our entire credit line in
advance, so the bankers couldn't detect a pattern of buying and
borrowing. We bought Gulf stock through Bear Stearns, headed by
one of Wall Street's best brokers, Ace Greenberg. Ace and I were
old Oklahoma friends. Money was transferred in aggregates of up
to $50 million from numbered bank accounts around the country
in a coded system so we wouldn't attract attention and drive the
stock up prematurely. We were getting smarter all the time and
were eventually going to get good at this game.

Once we were ready to make our takeover intentions known,
we set up a command post in a New York hotel and began working day and night. We took out newspaper ads to advise Gulf's
shareholders that we would pay a premium for their shares. As we

had expected, Gulf's management responded with righteous indignation but no real firepower. CEO Jimmy Lee cried that I had a history of "hit-and-run tactics," and my team and I were "cannibalizing" his company. CFO Harold Hammer was even tougher. "We've got to roll up our sleeves and hit him where it really smarts," he said. One of Gulf's hometown newspapers chimed in with an editorial: "Mesa chairman T. Boone Pickens expects primarily to cash in on Gulf's golden eggs, which are in the form of vast amounts of oil and gas. After obtaining the revenue there, he plans to slaughter the goose."

We upped our Gulf holdings to 13.2 percent. Lee and his team put on a show of resistance even while they were inviting potential merger partners to come to Pittsburgh. They would rather liquidate their company than be taken over. On October 31, 1983, we announced that we would lead a proxy fight over Gulf's proposal to move its state of incorporation to Delaware and to enact a stronger takeover defense. The battle with Gulf was in full force. They had hoped to push us back with this maneuver. This headline said it all:

GULF OIL VERSUS MR. PICKENS
THE WINNER TAKES $18.9 BILLION

It was followed by a lengthy subhead: "Can a Multi-Millionaire Texan Take Over Gulf Oil, a Company with $28 Billion in Annual Revenues? Boone Pickens Is Sure Trying. Gulf Could Buy Him Out for $1.5 Billion. But They Refuse. It Promises to Be One of the Roughest Battles to Hit Wall Street—and It Raises Some Important Questions."

Gulf's management upped the ante by spending millions in stockholders' money to launch an all-out war against us. They unleashed phone banks, public relations assaults, and private eyes to monitor our comings and goings. Since we were the largest shareholder in Gulf, we were effectively paying for the fight against ourselves. But that was corporate America.

Gulf filed lawsuits and tried to persuade U.S. senators to introduce legislation to stop oil company mergers. When the proxy votes were counted, Gulf's management won by a narrow margin. However, they could see the handwriting on the wall. They couldn't stand another vote. On Monday, March 5, 1984, after a five-month battle, Gulf entered into a merger agreement with Chevron. Chevron's offer was $80 a share. By then, most of Gulf's top executives had sold in the $50 range. Even then they hadn't realized the full value of the company. Shareholders that remained saw a $6.5 billion increase in the value of their shares. None of this would have been possible if Mesa and the Gulf Investors Group hadn't come onto the scene. Not long afterward, during a speech in Louisiana, a six-foot-five guy weighing about 270 picked me up and hugged me.

I asked him if he was a Gulf shareholder.

"You better believe it, bubba," he said. "I own ten thousand shares, and I appreciate what you did for me."

I told him I was glad it wasn't 100,000, or he'd have broken all my ribs.

It was the biggest deal of my life, one that would result in the largest corporate merger of all time: $13.2 billion. The deal changed the dynamics of mergers and acquisitions. As Gulf's largest shareholder, our Gulf Investors Group earned $760 million. Mesa netted $404 million—well over the $300 million we needed to put ourselves back on financially firm ground. For years, Gulf shareholders, including the Mellon family, had gotten the short end of the stick because of poor management. They considered us heroes for taking on one of the Seven Sisters—the largest oil companies in the nation—but it was not a total win for us. No question, though, it was a big victory.

Fifty arbitrageurs made $300 million on the Gulf deal because of our efforts. They hosted a dinner for me in Manhattan to show their appreciation. Mayor Ed Koch gave me a crystal Big Apple and thanked me for the estimated $50 million that our efforts brought to the city in legal fees and other services.

Takeover mania gripped America. New insider terminology became part of the 1980s lexicon. People began throwing around terms like *golden parachute* (special compensation for an executive fleeing a company), *white knight* (an individual or company that rescues a target company in a takeover fight and almost always added security to the CEO), *shark repellent* (extreme measures like changes in bylaws to keep a takeover at bay), and *poison pill* (a strategy to make a target company unattractive and ward off a takeover).

Defining me was tougher. "To many, he is a real-life J. R. Ewing, the ruthless but fascinating wheeler-dealer whom viewers of *Dallas* loved to hate—and sometimes secretly admired," proclaimed *Time* in a 1985 cover story. "To his victims, mostly entrenched corporate executives, he is a dangerous upstart, a sneaky poker player, a veritable rattlesnake in the woodpile. To his fans, though, he is a modern David, a champion of the little guy who can take on the Goliaths of Big Oil and more often than not gives them a costly whupping. T. (for Thomas) Boone Pickens, 56, has swept up like a twister out of Texas to become one of the most famous and controversial businessmen in the U.S. today."

In most accounts, I was inaccurately portrayed as a greenmailer or a Gordon Gekko, the double-dealer that Michael Douglas brought to life in his Oscar-winning performance in the movie *Wall Street*. Unlike Gekko, I did not believe that "greed is good." I simply believed that shareholders were being shortchanged by management and that the time had come to pull back the covers on the excesses of corporate America. Through our takeover attempts, my team and I introduced the concept that reigns supreme today—shareholder value. Our efforts increased this value in our target companies by at least $12 billion. "You would have to go back to the last century, to people like Jay Gould and Jim Fisk, to find someone who has had an equivalent impact on a major American industry," Joseph Fogg III of Morgan Stanley told *Time*. "Those two financiers reshaped U.S. railroads by forcing the consolidation of many different lines. Today Pickens is performing much the same feat in the energy industry."

I should have quit the takeover game after Gulf. I didn't. I was a folk hero at the time, and that should've been good enough. Instead of backing off, in late 1984 we targeted Phillips Petroleum. It was a street brawl or worse. Phillips not only unleashed the legal hounds on us, but they also marched out the citizens in the corporation's hometown of Bartlesville, Oklahoma, where I said I would move if we took over the company. I had lived there in 1951 when I'd worked for Phillips. The churches of Bartlesville were called upon to stage prayer vigils. Some townsfolk wore BooneBusters T-shirts. At one public meeting, four thousand people, including Phillips employees (but few outside shareholders), sang:

> There's gonna be a meeting at the old town hall tonight.
> And if they try to stop us, there's gonna be a fight.

We're gonna get our company out of this awful fix.

'Cause we don't want to change our name to Pickens 66.

In the end, Phillips executives folded like a three-dollar tent. They tried to buy us off with greenmail. We could have picked their pockets if we had been willing to take greenmail, but nobody in our camp was interested. When we wouldn't accept greenmail, Phillips offered to "sell" us an oil field for $100 million that was worth $200 million. Not interested in that either. I want to set the record straight: We never accepted greenmail in this deal or any other one. We had many opportunities but refused to take anything that wasn't offered to all shareholders.

Some 150,000 Phillips shareholders saw their stock go up $15 a share, a 40 percent increase and a market value enhancement of more than $2 billion in less than three months. The last time Phillips had had any excitement in the stock was when they'd discovered Echo Fisk in the North Sea. As one of Phillips's largest shareholders, we went home with an $89 million profit. We made some money, yet much less than we expected. The Phillips employee stock ownership plan (ESOP) was the big winner. They made more than $300 million. I'm still waiting for my thank-you note from this crowd.

Decades later, when I was inducted into the Oklahoma Hall of Fame, my good friend Burns Hargis, now president of Oklahoma State University, told the crowd, "Boone is such a loyal Oklahoman, he would have never moved Phillips out of Oklahoma as Conoco did. He may have moved it to Holdenville from Bartlesville, but they'd never have left Oklahoma."

IT WAS OBVIOUS, though, that Big Oil was tired of Boone Pickens and was intent on digging in and figuring out ways to fight me off. The major oil companies, whether I was against them or not, were all against me. Finally I figured out that I wasn't going to take over a major oil company. The oil company executives and boards of directors just wouldn't let me do it. If I ever became the CEO of a major oil company and changed the culture of the company to make it more successful, their jobs would all be threatened.

I heard that the CEO of one of the majors said, "Boone could never run a major oil company." That was a laugh. If some of those guys could run a major, I damn sure could have done it—better than they could. It would have been easy if I could ever have gotten my hands on the controls. However, it finally dawned on me: *Hey, everybody is against you in this industry.* I truly felt that way.

Mesa's last Big Oil target was Unocal, then the twelfth-largest oil company in the United States. We made a bid of $54 a share for 64 million shares, which was enough to give us majority ownership. Unocal countered by offering $72 a share for 50 million shares of its stock. This was designed to keep shareholders from tendering to Mesa. The coup de grace was that Unocal was excluding Mesa from participating in the offer, a clear violation of the legal principle stating that all shareholders must be treated equally.

We sued Unocal in Delaware and Los Angeles for excluding us from the stock offer. We were sure the courts would rule in our favor. The chancery court in Delaware did exactly that. Then Delaware's Supreme Court reversed that decision, and Unocal's plan to cut us out of the deal was upheld. It was a Pyrrhic victory for management, one that *Time* singled out as much for the way it violated shareholder rights as its senseless expense:

> The victory over Pickens was a costly one for Unocal. The company's elaborate takeover defenses, including the

huge stock buy-back, will leave Unocal saddled with a long-term debt of $5.4 billion, compared with only $1.3 billion before the fight. This prompted Standard & Poor's . . . to downgrade Unocal's credit rating. To support the massive debt, the company will probably have to trim back its oil exploration and perhaps even sell some assets to raise cash. . . .

The Delaware court decision, however, struck many financial experts as a potentially dangerous step. Felix Rohatyn, a partner of the Lazard Frères investment firm and one of the most outspoken critics of Pickens-style hostile takeovers, blasted the decision because it violated the principle of investor equality. Said he: "This creates two tiers of stockholders. The vaccine is as bad as the disease. It's crazy."

Although Unocal's chairman, Fred Hartley, crowed that he had defeated us and had cost Mesa $100 million, when all the smoke cleared we actually netted an $83 million profit on our Unocal attempt. Besides our profit, moral vindication came in the summer of 1986, when the SEC finally came out with a ruling that exclusionary offers such as Unocal's were unacceptable because they discriminated against selected stockholders.

My game plan with Gulf, Phillips, and Unocal hadn't been to take on Big Oil. Hell, that hadn't been my role. My role had been to make money for the stockholders of Mesa, and the opportunity had presented itself because Big Oil's management had done a lousy job. If Mesa could become a stockholder and I could upgrade those assets, I would make all shareholders a profit.

There's no question that of all the deals we were involved in, the

Unocal case had the most far-reaching legal consequences. It received the most attention in contemporary business courses. In fact, I now have a new generation of college students in business courses asking me, "Are you *that* Boone Pickens?" In 1997, *Directors & Boards* magazine named Mesa-Unocal [*Unocal Corp. v Mesa Petroleum Co., 493 A.2d 946 (Del. 1985)*] as one of the top ten cases having the most impact upon corporate law in this country. In its decision, which has become known as "the Unocal test for boards of directors," the Delaware court ruled that a board of directors can attempt to prevent takeovers only when there is a threat to corporate policy, and even then the board can use only tactics that are reasonable in proportion to the threat. "The ultimate goal of the corporate governance movement has been to stimulate corporate management to create the kind of superior financial results that enhance 'shareholder value,' " the section devoted to the Unocal decision begins. This was exactly our speech for years. That's what management is hired to do. Fortunately, even when we lost a war, the stockholders prospered by what we did.

We had made tremendous profits from our efforts, but I was concerned about the deteriorating investment environment in the United States. Owners and shareholders were unorganized, intimidated, and treated like second-class citizens even though they were putting up the money to finance corporate America. Back then, it was estimated that approximately 20 percent of the U.S. population owned shares in corporations. They had an average age of forty-four, a yearly household income of $37,000, and a stock portfolio of $6,000. They weren't rich—and they weren't represented. Until the summer of 1986. That's when I launched the United Shareholders Association (USA), a national lobbying group dedicated to giving American shareholders a platform and a voice. My name was out front with USA. To finance its costs, I donated the $1.5 million advance from my first book, *Boone,* as well as proceeds from my speaking fees, which ranged from $20,000 to $100,000 a speech. Our supporters included billionaire financier Carl Icahn, Cincinnati businessman Carl Lindner, and Dallas financier Harold Simmons. Our first year's budget was $1.3 million.

"Look at the Business Roundtable," I said at the press conference in Washington kicking off USA. "It's made up of the two hundred largest corporations in America. Who goes to their meetings? The CEOs. They meet several times a year here in Washington behind closed doors. Do you think they are working in our interests? I don't think so."

We were ready to launch the attack on corporate America. Corporate America came out swinging. In the spring of 1985, Drew Lewis, then the CEO of Union Pacific Railroad (and who later served as secretary of transportation under President Ronald Reagan), called and said he needed to see me. I invited him out to the ranch, picked him up at the airport, and took him to dinner. He had just returned from a meeting of the Business Roundtable. Lewis told me that a prominent CEO was the lead spokesman and had addressed the Roundtable, saying, "Boone Pickens is dangerous to corporate America." Then he'd asked for contributions to take me down.

"He said he wanted fifty thousand dollars from each of the members," Lewis reported.

Lewis hadn't anted up, though most of the other members had. They'd collected almost $10 million for their war chest. I was in the crosshairs. "They're coming after you," he said. They had ordered their respective public relations representatives to dig up dirt on me and to spread it.

"Who handles your PR?" Lewis asked.

"I do."

"Well, you're the worst I've ever seen. My advice to you is to dig a hole, get in it, and pull it on top of yourself."

Damned if they didn't do exactly what Drew Lewis predicted. They tried to bury me, but they were too late. In February 1992, USA launched a one-million-dollar, fifty-state campaign to support SEC action on executive compensation and other reforms. USA scored a number of major victories, attracted sixty-five thousand members, and sparked a national dialogue on corporate governance issues. By 1993, we had done the job we'd set out to do: corporate culture had changed so that shareholder concerns were now more integrated into business decisions and planning. We decided to shut down USA. It may be the only successful lobbying group to ever go out of business.

> ***Booneism #6:*** *In a deal between friends, there's no place for a wolverine.*

I GAVE UP hunting elephants in the oil industry with the Unocal deal in 1985. There were deals after that but not for me. Mesa had grown to become one of America's largest independent oil and gas companies, with 80 percent of our reserves in natural gas.

In 1985 we changed Mesa's corporate structure to a master limited partnership, which we believed was the premier structure for the future of the oil industry. It was similar to our idea of the Mesa Royalty Trust back in 1979. We were twenty years ahead of our time. The deal turned our shareholders into limited partners with the best possible tax circumstances. Converting to a limited partnership made Mesa stronger than ever, with a market capitalization of $2 billion. We had another $500 million of transactions in process. In 1986 we acquired Pioneer Corporation, a West Texas exploration and production company, for $800 million. We paid for the purchase by exchanging Mesa Limited Partnership Preference "A" units for Pioneer stock. Holders of "A" units were guaranteed distributions of $1.50 per unit annually until mid-1991, when the units would be converted into common units. Because the price of gas went down, this guaranteed distribution was a killer. If Hugoton was the best deal I've ever done, the Pioneer acquisition was the worst, so bad that it makes me think of another critical learning experience.

My grandmother had six small rental houses. She said if I would mow the lawns, she would furnish the mower. She asked me to bid on the job for the summer. I didn't know what she meant. She explained that if I came up with a price for mowing the six lawns that was acceptable to her, she would pay me that price and we would have a verbal contract.

I offered to mow the lawns for ten cents a lawn, thinking that would be a lot of money. At that time, my paper route was only twenty-eight papers, and I was paid a penny a paper for a total of twenty-eight cents. A dime a lawn represented quite a bonus over throwing papers—or so it seemed. My grandmother agreed to the price, so I started mowing. Then it started raining. It would rain two days, then we would have sun for five days. I could see the grass growing—and growing. I hadn't looked at the job very closely. I hadn't realized the lawns were as big as they were, or what a rainy summer would do to me.

"This was a very bad summer, and you made a bad deal," my grandmother told me. I couldn't help agreeing. "I'm going to help you out, Sonny," she said.

"Grandmother, what are you going to do for me?"

"I'll sharpen the lawn mower."

"Is that all?"

"Sonny, these are the kinds of things that you will never forget," she said. "I can assure you, the next time you bid on a job, you'll give a lot more thought to it." There was no easy way out of my bad deal with Pioneer. Nobody sharpened my lawn mower. Pioneer was the sorriest and last deal I ever made.

My mother had passed away in 1977 of an inoperable brain tumor. After her funeral, my father said to me, "Don't leave me here in Amarillo." I said, "Dad, don't worry. I'll stay here with you." After my father's death in 1988, I was free to go. The next year I moved to Dallas and took Mesa with me. I also moved my parents to the Holdenville cemetery. I now had no reason ever to return to Amarillo. I felt I had overstayed in a small town. My detractors said I would never like it in Dallas. They said I'd be a small fish in a big pond instead of a big fish in a small one. How wrong they were. I love Dallas. Not only has the city accepted me with open arms but I also soon realized the business significance of being headquartered in one of the country's major metropolitan areas. The deal flow, the contacts, the travel—everything is so much easier in a big city. The *Dallas Morning News* is a welcome improvement over the *Amarillo Globe-News*.

After I moved to Dallas, Mesa became the target of a takeover staged by my former CFO, David Batchelder. It had to have been one of the three biggest surprises of my life. We had a lot in common. We both had gone to Oklahoma State University (albeit twenty years apart), where we'd both been in the same fraternity (Sigma Alpha Epsilon). He had come to Mesa as a young accountant and left with a lot of experience and an $8 million net worth. The only downside to his ten-year career at Mesa was that I'd beat him regularly in racquetball and cards. In December 1994, seven years after he'd left Mesa, David came to me and said that one of his clients, Dennis Washington, had acquired a $15 million stake in Mesa. The alleged West Coast billionaire Marvin Davis had also bought shares. David said we should sell the company or face a proxy fight.

Batchelder got a lot of media coverage. "The student goes after the teacher" was an irresistible story peg in the business press, but it didn't amount to much. Batchelder had overestimated the value of Mesa to Dennis Washington and Marvin Davis. They quickly figured this out and exited the deal in August 1995.

By 1996 our stock price had dropped to $2⅝ per share. We'd been talking for months about alternatives. *Could we raise more equity? Who might be possible equity players? Should we take Mesa into bankruptcy?*

"Let's go to New York," urged my friend Doug Miller, CEO of Coda Energy, Inc. "You can get the money to recapitalize the company."

I had gotten so down on myself at that point that I just couldn't act. Looking back, I probably could have raised the money. Instead, we kept working with Lehman Brothers to find a buyer. After thirteen months without any results, I decided to look for a bailout in the form of an equity infusion.

"If you're ever in trouble, call me," Richard Rainwater had told me over the years.

I had known Richard for a long time. I called him in October 1995 while he was at Canyon Ranch, the Tucson health spa. Richard had recently married Darla Moore, a tough-talking, savvy bankruptcy specialist who had become the highest-paid woman in banking after joining Chemical Bank. He called her "Little Precious" and described her as "the best investment I ever made." Other people called her the DIP Queen, for her specialty—debtor-inpossession financing to companies facing Chapter 11 bankruptcy protection. Darla pioneered DIP financing during her tenure at Chemical Bank. Along with being Richard's wife, she was also his business partner, the bad cop to his good cop. As the CEO of Rainwater, Inc., Darla handled the daily work of the company. She liked to give people the impression that she pissed ice water, and that was a good read. I eventually flew out to Canyon Ranch, and Richard and I talked about his making an equity infusion into Mesa.

We finally hammered out a deal in which Richard would put $133 million into Mesa. Mesa shareholders would add another $132 million in a rights offering to recapitalize the company. In addition to his equity, Richard would get four seats out of the seven on the board. I controlled three seats, meaning Richard could outvote me with his four. The company would be in his control. At this point, I still wanted to believe that I could lead the company I had founded forty years earlier out of its problems.

Before the deal was finalized, the Rainwaters called for a meeting at their home in Montecito, California. "Don't get pissed off and resign," my attorney Bobby Stillwell said as we flew out to meet them. My longtime ally and one of my closest friends, Bobby had been my legal counsel since the early 1960s. He knows me better than almost anybody. On the day we went to meet the Rainwaters, he knew I wasn't myself, and he didn't know what I was going to do. If I resigned, I wouldn't get the severance offered to all departing Mesa employees. "It's better for you if they fire you," he told me.

"The Toughest Babe in Business" was the cover line of a *Fortune* story about Darla—with some references to me—that would be published about a year after our meeting in Montecito. The article described her as "a cross between the Terminator and Kim Basinger, with a wicked South Carolina drawl." Her friend Martha Stewart, no shrinking violet herself, called her "a cutthroat killer." On the cover, Darla gazed into the camera with a deadly stare, beside this subtitle: "Darla Moore married Richard Rainwater, tripled his wealth, axed Boone Pickens, and pushed Rick Scott out at Columbia/HCA. Stay tuned."

After reading "The Toughest Babe in Business" cover story with Darla's comments about me — "I tried to be as tactful as I could, but tact doesn't come easily to me" — I sent her a letter. "Darla, thanks for a great article. Next time I see you in New York, let's have a drink at The Plaza. I want to tell you the story about the scorpion and the frog."

She never responded. Instead, she forwarded my letter to *Fortune,* whose writer called me to ask if they could publish it. "Yes, if you put an asterisk by it saying the letter Boone Pickens wrote to Darla Moore was forwarded to the magazine by Darla Moore," I said. "I bet you ten dollars that she won't let you say it came from her."

The writer called me back. "You were right. By the way, tell me the story about the scorpion and the frog."

> The floodwater is coming up and a scorpion's going to drown. The scorpion asks the frog for a ride to higher ground.
>
> "Oh no, scorpion, you're so treacherous, I would be afraid to give you a ride anywhere," said the frog.
>
> "No, frog, if you save my life, I'll never do anything to harm you," pled the scorpion.
>
> "OK, well, get on my back," said the frog, and he swam with the scorpion on his back to dry land. Just before the scorpion got off of his back, he stung the frog.

"Scorpion, I saved your life. You stung me, and now I'm going to die. Why did you do that to somebody who saved your life?" moaned the dying frog.

"Hell, frog, that's just the kind of a son of a bitch I am."

When Bobby and I landed at the Santa Barbara Airport, Richard and Darla were there to meet us. I remember thinking, *God Almighty, I can't believe they both came out to greet me.* Then it hit me. They'd come out to see our airplane, an old Falcon 20. They wanted to get onboard and take a look around. I guess they thought they were going to get a big plane with the deal.

We went to their house, and the Rainwaters switched into their good-cop–bad-cop routine. Richard was his usual effervescent, somewhat uncomfortable self. I could tell he wanted no part of what was about to happen and wanted to quickly pass me off to Darla. Richard went off with Bobby, while Darla ushered me out to the patio with a glass of iced tea. She made it clear she felt I hadn't kept up with the times in the oil and gas industry. She said something about my reputation being a problem. "You know we can't do this deal with your being the CEO," she said.

"That's fine," I said. "It's like starting the season with a sixty-eight-year-old quarterback. You may end up with one, but you don't start with one."

That was it: less than half an hour, and Bobby and I were gone. I was finished at Mesa, and I wanted to be finished. I was ready to move on to something else.

IRVING, TEXAS, February 29, 1996—MESA Inc. and Rainwater Inc., a company owned by Fort Worth, Texas, investor Richard Rainwater and managed by Darla D. Moore and

Kenneth A. Hersh, announced today they have signed a letter of intent to raise $265 million of equity in connection with a refinancing of Mesa's debt. Rainwater and affiliates will purchase $133 million of convertible preferred stock, provide a standby commitment for a $132 million rights offering of convertible preferred stock and assist in the refinancing of all Mesa's debt. The MESA/Rainwater transaction caps a 13-month effort by the company to strengthen its financial position.

—Business Wire

The deal would get Mesa back doing what it did best: finding oil and gas. During the transition, there were several unusual events that took place. We had made a deal, and we were going to stick with it by turning over a top-notch operation. We had a seasoned staff that knew exactly what to do. I saw it as a very simple transition.

I agreed to stay on and run the company until we found a new CEO. It was at this time that Richard brought in Ken Hersh to oversee his investment. Just as soon as Hersh showed up, problems started. Hersh was in his early thirties and had very little managerial experience. One thing that was pretty obvious was that Hersh felt he didn't have anything to learn from any of us. Things got squirrelly pretty fast. He got the idea that if they cut out the fourteenth floor—meaning my floor—they could cut overhead by $5 million. We were already cut down to the bone, but they wanted more cuts. We made the cuts.

Meanwhile, Hersh questioned everything and everybody. Here he was, looking after Richard's $133 million investment, and what did he want to know? Whether Mesa rented or owned the plants in the office. One of our guys described him as a young robin: all mouth and asshole. He went to Mesa's vice president of public affairs, Andrew Littlefair, who had come to us in 1987 from the Reagan White House, and said, "Well, you got yourself a fiefdom here. What is it exactly that you do?"

At the first board meeting, Darla Moore followed up on that thought. She had comments to make, which obviously came from Ken Hersh. "Let's get rid of Littlefair," she said. "Why don't we fire him?"

Andrew Littlefair was one of our key guys. He was very productive and has since gone on to become the CEO of our publicly traded Clean Energy Fuels company, which sells natural gas as a transportation fuel. Firing him was a ludicrous suggestion, which the board immediately brushed off. Somehow Rainwater and Hersh had gotten the idea that there was a lot of waste at Mesa. There wasn't. It was well run and had good people doing good jobs.

There's a lesson to be learned here. Richard and I were friends when we made our deal. By the time it fully played out, we weren't. I never understood why both sides don't work together to make an easy transition when they make a deal. All too often there's a wolverine in the deal. Wolverines piss on everything they can't eat. Right or wrong, that's how I saw Darla Moore and Ken Hersh. And that's why I believe the transition got bungled.

Booneism #7: *You are pissing in my ear and telling me it's raining outside.*

RON BASSETT AND I had just made $20 million for the company trading energy futures. Then a loan officer at Chase called. He told me the bankers felt that they couldn't go on the road show for their equity and debt offering if Mesa was involved in commodities.

"What are you talking about?" I asked.

"Well, if you lost everything in the commodity play you're in, you would lose $150 million," he said.

"Yeah, but for that to happen, natural gas would have to go to zero. Natural gas can't go to zero."

"We just can't do it, Boone," the loan officer said.

I told him how well we had done in our trading activities over the previous decade, and that all of it had been fully disclosed in our annual report and other financial filings.

"Well, we're not going to do it," he said. "And you've got to get out in the next thirty days."

"I'll tell you what," I said. "Look at your watch, and we'll be out in fifteen minutes."

Then I hung up. There was no question that these were orders from Rainwater. In fifteen minutes, Mesa was out of the commodities market. Mesa board member John Cox and I had a side-by-side account with Mesa that gave our directors a great deal of confidence. Cox and I had our own money in the same positions Mesa was in. John and I didn't liquidate our positions, and we made another $15 million by staying. Mesa would have made twice that if they had stayed.

Not long after that the loan officer returned to my office with more news from the bankers. He told me that they couldn't restructure the company if I was CEO.

"That's fine," I said. "I've already had this conversation with Darla." Somehow, the Chase banker and, apparently, the Rainwaters couldn't understand that I was ready to go. I had been there for forty years, so they felt that getting me out would be a struggle.

I told the banker I'd be gone as soon as a replacement CEO was found.

"Like that?" he said.

"Just like that."

I was still the largest individual shareholder. I wasn't going to leave until we had a CEO, and I was afraid Rainwater was going to turn it over to Hersh. And Hersh was too short for the job.

A DECADE LATER, in 2007, I was at Bob's Steak and Chop House. That same Chase loan officer was at the bar having a drink with my friend Doug Miller. Doug came over to the table.

"This guy has something he wants to tell you."

"Is it worth hearing?"

"Yeah, you oughta go over there and hear what he has to say."

So I did.

"I'd like to clear something up that I've been carrying around for ten years," he began. "Rainwater told me that I had to tell you that we couldn't recapitalize the company with you as CEO. That was bullshit. We could have done it with anybody as CEO."

He exhaled.

"Now I don't have to think about that anymore."

BUT THINGS BEGAN to go better for the company in the first quarter of 1996. Gas moved up to $2.26 per Mcf, and we had our first profitable quarter since 1989. Up jumped the good cop.

"Why don't you stay?" Richard asked me, adding that he'd already quit looking for my successor.

"No, I'm leaving."

I knew by then what I was going to do, and it didn't include Mesa. My new business would be the one that the Rainwaters didn't want: commodities trading, building on our success in the energy markets, the ten-year run that had begun in 1986. I was so certain of it that I had hired five people from Mesa and leased office space. "I've already got another office," I told Richard.

The Mesa executives, Rainwater, and Hersh were preparing to go on a road show to sell the "new Mesa." *How could it be the new anything with me still there?* So I called Richard in New York and asked him to meet me at the Teterboro Airport in New Jersey on June 12, 1996. I brought things to a conclusion. Richard agreed to honor the standard severance package that was going to all Mesa employees. I think he was elated to take out the founder of the company and its leader for forty years for only $5 million. We announced my departure the next day in the following letter to employees:

> Richard Rainwater and I have agreed to work together to locate the best possible CEO for Mesa. I will remain on the job until that process is complete. After that I will remain one of Mesa's largest shareholders and will continue as a member of the board of directors.
>
> After 40 years, I believe some personal observations are in order. Mesa has come a long way since 1956 when I founded the company with a $2,500 stake.
>
> Mesa has operated worldwide and drilled more than 4,800 wells with a success rate of 75 percent. We went to Canada in 1959 with $35,000 and sold out 20 years later for $610 million. We have produced more than 3 trillion cubic feet of natural gas—the equivalent of 500 million barrels of oil. We have distributed nearly $2 billion to stockholders in dividends and distributions.
>
> As I look back on the past 40 years, I take pride in what we have built. This could not have been done without

your hard work. I hope you know how much I appreciate
your contributions. This has been a fantastic 40 years for
me. The people I have worked with and the deals I have
been involved in I will never forget.

In July I addressed the Mesa annual meeting for the last time. It
was a sad day. "I don't spend a lot of time looking over my shoulder," I told one reporter. But it was a tough speech to deliver, and
one writer noted that I seemed to be "fighting back tears."

The *Dallas Morning News* published an interview with me on
my last day on the job. In the picture that ran over the story, I was
leaning back in my chair with my feet up on the desk. There was a
hole in my sole. The week before I left Mesa, I had undergone a
colonoscopy, moved out of my home, and filed for divorce. Losing
Mesa hurt the most. Still, I always look on the bright side. That weekend, I went to play golf at Castle Pines with my old friends John Cox,
Bobby Stillwell (my lawyer), and Dee Kelly (John's lawyer). After the
game, we were sitting on the porch, having a drink and enjoying the
weather. "You know, guys, when you get down to it, I think that I'm
the luckiest guy in the world," I said. "I'm sitting here. My health is
good. I'm with friends. Your health is good. And I'd like to drink a
toast to the four of us. We're the luckiest guys in the world."

John and I had gone through quite a bit together. He'd always
been with me, whether good times or bad. This time he didn't go
along with me.

"I don't get it, Boone," he said. "Your business is terrible. You've
taken some big financial losses. And you're in the middle of what's
going to be a nasty divorce. And you don't have a job. And you
think you're the luckiest guy in the world. I think you may qualify
as the dumbest."

In August, Mesa brought Jon Brumley, formerly chief executive at Cross Timbers Oil, out of retirement and named him CEO. I had recommended Brumley for the job. With my three votes on the board, I would have plenty to say about who the new CEO would be. Nobody would take the job without unanimous approval. Brumley was an old friend of mine and a fraternity brother of Bobby Stillwell's at the University of Texas. I had a two-hour, one-on-one meeting with him, and Jon said, "I'll take the job, but I have to be CEO and chairman of the board."

"Don't worry. I'm tired of being chairman," I replied. And that was that.

In August 1997, Mesa merged with Parker & Parsley Petroleum Co. to create the nation's third-largest independent oil company: Pioneer Natural Resources. The merger gave their stock a real boost, but I thought it was a short-term move. Long-term, it was not a good deal for Mesa shareholders. Not long afterward I sold my stock at $34 and resigned from the board. Within a year the stock had dropped to $5 but has since rebounded.

With the merger, the Mesa name disappeared from the company that had borne it for more than forty years. When Pioneer gave up the Mesa name, we were quick to file for it, using it in our new ventures, including Mesa Water and Mesa Power, now working to build the world's largest wind farm in the Texas Panhandle. The Mesa name is synonymous with forty years of my career. Like me, it has plenty of time left.

My severance would turn out to be peanuts compared to what the Rainwater team let us take with us. First, our trading operation. From 1986 to 1996, we had been profitable ten straight years. The trades my longtime associate Ron Bassett and I did at Mesa covered all general and administrative costs: $150 million in total. As someone who prides himself on looking at the big picture, the long-term view, I should have changed our business plan and quit looking for oil and gas when the finding costs got too high and the prospects weren't there, instead concentrating on the futures market. Now I would.

The second business we got was the natural gas fueling company. I bought the fueling business from Mesa for $1.1 million in April 1997, in a deal that included a note receivable of $2.1 million, which meant they virtually paid me to take the company. We named it Pickens Fuel Corp. Now called Clean Energy Fuels (NASDAQ: CLNE), the fueling business has 185 stations, compared with just two when we bought it. Its market cap is now twice the size of Mesa's when we left. They figured neither the commodities trading business nor the natural gas fueling business was worth much. They figured wrong.

Before I left, the company gave me a farewell dinner at Bob's Steak and Chop House. The Rainwaters and their short-boy Hersh did not receive invitations. Brumley gave me a good-bye gift— *Boomtown Drifters,* an oil painting by my good friend G. Harvey, which had hung in the lobby of the Mesa offices for years. People gave toasts and speeches. One or two people cried. I got up and said a few words about how much I loved the company and appreciated everyone's hard work and dedication. I didn't mention the word *retirement.* There would be no retirement for me, and I had gotten over the prospect of any tears. I was seriously into my new life at that point. I always said Mesa's greatest asset was its people, so when I left to start my new business, I took a few of their best.

In the late afternoon of my last day, I looked out the window one last time. I was sixty-eight years old. I'd always wondered how it would end for me at Mesa. Would I retire quietly? Would I be carried out in a parade? Or dragged out in a box?

I'd known this day would come. I had decided many years earlier that when it was over, it was over. No hanging around with the title of chairman. No token office in the company headquarters. A long time ago, I came to realize the power that change brings. Because with change comes challenge. So leaving Mesa wasn't an end but the opportunity for a new beginning. When one door closes, another opens. Before turning off the lights for the last time and heading to my temporary home in the Four Seasons Hotel, I stood in an emptying office flooded with memories. I kept thinking how far we had come—and how far we had fallen. I contemplated what had happened, what hadn't happened, and what should have happened. It was all just a warm-up for what was yet to come.

"You leave like you came in," I always said. So at exactly 6:00 p.m. on my last day, I turned out the lights and walked out the door. My longtime assistant, Sally Geymüller, was also packed up and ready to go. She had been with Mesa since she was seventeen, starting as a part-timer in the central records department before becoming my right arm.

"How do you feel about leaving?" she asked.

"I'm ready to get the hell out of here," I said.

She clenched her fists and flashed a wide and brilliant smile.

"I am too!" she said. "Let's get the hell out of here!"

As we left, neither of us could imagine what awaited us on the other side. I felt optimistic about my future. My next act had begun.

CHAPTER 3

Starting Over

Booneism #8: I have always believed that it's important to show a new look periodically. Predictability can lead to failure.

September 1996: BP Capital, Preston Center, Dallas, Texas

M Y NEW BUSINESS opened quietly at 3:30 a.m. on September 27, 1996. We moved into our new offices in the middle of the night. It's not as bad as it sounds; we just couldn't use the elevators to move our furniture and files during the day. Nights and weekends were fine. We wanted to see the markets open the next day.

It was just me and five former Mesa employees: Ron Bassett, my longtime associate; Sally Geymüller, my assistant of twenty-seven years; Denise Delile, our secretary; Bob Kultgen, accountant/trader; and Hondo McKinney, junior accountant. The six of us stood on the threshold of what would become the greatest business adventure of our lives.

Do what you know best. That's what I've always believed. Since I'm a foot wide and a mile deep on the subject of oil and gas, my new business would be built on what I knew best. When we left

Mesa, we hadn't raised $1 in seed money for our new venture. Our greatest capital was the shared belief that our best years were ahead of us.

The blood, guts, and feathers of what would happen next is one hell of a story. It goes far beyond mere dollars and cents. It would prove that age is meaningless in some instances, and that opportunity in America is endless. We are allowed second, third, fourth, and fifth acts, and who knows how many more. Resurgence instead of retirement. We would achieve such success trading commodities and equities at BP Capital in such a short time that people would say we made it look easy. However, it took a lifetime of hard work and constant learning to acquire the knowledge, expertise, and gut feeling to be able to accomplish what I've done in the last decade. And maybe a little luck. I was going to build a new life and a new business with the greatest capital anyone can have: experience. While building a lucrative new business, I discovered a second life and a second wind.

It was a great personal test, and it raised a lot of questions for me, at sixty-eight. Not once did I ever consider retirement. It's not in my DNA. I'd been at one place for forty years, where I built a hell of a company and a great team. Could I do it all over again from scratch? Sure, there were seeds of doubt. Going from four hundred people to six—it was a new day for me.

As Bobby Stillwell likes to say, "Boone has been in the prime of his life three times." This time, I would find a way to enhance my business career and my personal life through my continuing commitment to physical fitness and staying on top of the ever-changing oil and gas business. The rewards are beyond anything I experienced as a "young" man. I also learned that the direction of success is never straight up. Sometimes in the oil business, you have to drill deep to reach your objective. If that fails, you reach a point where you think all is lost and there is nothing there. Most people, both in business and in life, surrender. As a result, they fall short of their dreams, opportunities, and potential. I learned that if you never give up, if you push through the resistance and keep driving for what you want, you will ultimately achieve rewards beyond any you had hoped for. Because down deep, just beyond the hard, tough spot we all have found ourselves in, there awaits the opportunity to become stronger, more successful, and more fulfilled than you have ever imagined. Never, never, never give up.

I was in that hard, tough spot in the fall of 1996.

BP Capital had leased a modest office, which we outfitted with used furniture and off-the-shelf computers to link us to the financial markets. I had my desk and chair that I'd taken from Mesa and a computer and a telephone. These were the new tools of the trade that I would use to launch my second career, in which the riches were locked not deep underground but in the complex world of the commodities and equities markets. We had off-loaded the operations side of the business in leaving Mesa. We were now hunting with a rifle, not a shotgun. I was alone with only five employees dependent on me and Murdock, my one-year-old papillon. I liked that feeling. No baggage. I'd traded the corporate jet for "the company plane," as the ads of Southwest Airlines say. It really was a new life.

"The Old Man Makes a Comeback." It's an imaginary headline that has captivated me for years. I had to make a comeback—and who doesn't love the idea of that? I didn't care for the tennis star Jimmy Connors until he was forty. When he was young, I found him cocky and overbearing. Yet I found myself pulling for Connors when he was forty, humbled and fighting back.

You can stay around as long as you stay active—and, of course, have a plan. A fool with a plan can outsmart a genius with no plan any day. We had a plan, and, considering our performance, I thought it was a good one. One other thing: we weren't fools. I remember thinking, *We can do it.* It was sort of like a favorite photograph, the one of New York Giants quarterback Y. A. Tittle, down on both knees after a hard game. His face was bloodied, but he looked like he could get up and lead his team for another quarter. I felt like Tittle, both in the way I had been beaten up and the way I was ready to get going again.

I knew we would be successful. I always think that, having had success before, but I didn't know how successful we could be starting over; I'd never had that experience. I remember thinking, *If we could make a couple million dollars a year, I'd be satisfied.* It would be comeback enough.

I figured I could raise $50 million to $100 million to launch the BP Capital Energy Fund. I figured wrong. Outside of my team and a loyal circle of friends, investors weren't lining up to become a part of my new venture. Most of them thought I was over the hill, a has-been who had seen better days. It came home to me that the fourth quarter was already under way and I had to make a comeback.

I WAS ORIGINALLY introduced to the commodities market with cattle. In 1969, after Mesa acquired Hugoton, America's appetite for steak was enormous. The Texas Panhandle was becoming an epicenter of beef. Its custom feedlots, where livestock were fattened, were replacing traditional Midwestern farm feedlots. These custom feedlots produced substantial cash flow that, in turn, would help feed Mesa's ever-increasing appetite for drilling in the Gulf of Mexico. We decided to get into the feedlot business.

Within three years, Mesa became America's second-largest cattle feeder. We had 160,000 head in three feed yards. Mesa also owned grain elevators, a trucking operation, and farmland. We leased 100,000 acres of ranch land. I was at a party one night when a strong wind swept up the stench from one of the feedlots and carried it into town. "That smells like shit!" a half-drunk woman said to me. "It may smell like shit to you, but it smells like money to me," I replied.

It quickly became clear to me that the most liquid market for cattle wasn't selling beef on the hoof but buying and selling live cattle futures on the Chicago Mercantile Exchange. I had begun trading agricultural commodities—cattle, corn, pork bellies—for my personal account. Mesa was leasing offices on the fifth floor of a building above a brokerage firm. I talked the brokerage people downstairs into running a wire up to my office so I could get the commodity and stock quotes. The quote machine was a simple gadget with keys that looked like an adding machine. You would punch the symbol of the commodity or stock you were interested in and the price would come up on paper tape. Today we use a state-of-the-art Bloomberg trading system. Back then, we relied on whatever we could get.

There's nothing like a commodities play for consistent action. Doing it successfully calls for accurate analysis, the nerve to take risks, and the ability to act. Investing in the commodities market plays to my strengths. Once you've made a decision, you know pretty fast whether you have succeeded. This is no place for an excitable person. You've got to stay cool.

During the early 1970s run-up in cattle prices, I parlayed $34,000 in live cattle futures into a $6.6 million gain in six months. My strategy was the same as today: staying current on every possible source of information, investing on the fundamentals of supply and demand, and sticking with my conviction over the long haul. I also reinvested all of my profits, thereby greatly increasing the number of contracts I held. Some might call this pyramiding. I call it staying with your long-term analysis.

Near the end of that run, I was playing in the Canadian Oilman's golf tournament in Banff, Alberta. On the first day of the tournament, I was on the course when the price for live cattle collapsed. After losing a million bucks in a few hours, I figured it was time to take the remaining profit and get out. However, the market had closed. The next morning I was ready to put in the sell order, but the phones were out in Banff Springs and tee time was 11:00 a.m. By the time I got off the course at 4:00 p.m., the market was closed again. Another million lost.

The next morning the phones were down again. "You look like you've got something on your mind," my opponent said. He was right. I took another million-dollar hit on the third day, finally getting out of the market with a $3.6 million profit. Very expensive tournament—and I didn't win it, either.

By early 1973, a five-cents-per-pound drop in the price of live cattle could have cost Mesa $8 million. A lot of the cattle were in our limited partnerships, and the limited partners were responsible for losses up to $25 per head. This left us with enough exposure to concern our Wall Street analysts. I had a hunch, based mostly on instinct, that they were right. I decided to cut our exposure. How? By hedging.

Hedging is a method for reducing your risk in a market by locking in a sale price. If you own the physical commodity, you take a futures position short. That way your exposure is reduced or eliminated. Any changes in the value of the physical market should be offset by changes in the value of the futures position. They were locked together.

Of course, some people think that trading in commodities is like playing poker. "That's gambling!" according to Tom Herrick, a Marlboro Man look-alike who ran Mesa's cattle operation for a brief period of time. I told him gambling was when you were not hedged. The days of full feedlots and easy profits were over.

In the end, the cattle business was not a successful venture for Mesa. We took our losses, sold our feed yards, and got out. What we learned in hedging cattle carried over into the incredibly profitable business of trading energy futures. It was another learning experience that would pay dividends in the future.

Then, in 1983, a big door opened for us.

The New York Mercantile Exchange was originally organized as the Butter and Cheese Exchange of New York and began commodities trading in 1872. Now the NYMEX was going to start trading crude oil futures. There was no question we were going to be a player at some point.

> **Booneism #9:** My mother once told me, "Son, you talk too much. You should listen more. You don't even know who the enemy is."

TO LAUNCH THE BP Capital Energy Fund in the fall of 1996, I had to pass a National Futures Association exam to become a commodity pool operator. I started studying right after we moved into our new offices. Once I felt ready, I made the appointment to take the test. You start at nine in the morning and have to finish it in six hours. Afterward, they tell you immediately whether you passed or failed. Ron Bassett and our trader Bob Kultgen had passed the test their first time.

How hard could this be?

I went into a room full of people who were getting ready to take the test, and this young guy came up to me. "Aren't you T. Boone Pickens?" he asked.

"Yep, that's right," I said. "Nice to meet you."

"Gosh, what are you doing here?"

"I'm taking the test."

"Taking the test?" he said. "I thought you wrote the book!"

About that time the instructor asked everyone to sit down at a computer, where the test would be given. I struggled from the start. I had to use a calculator, which I never do. Pretty soon somebody finished, then somebody else, and soon the room emptied out and it was just me.

I took all the time allotted, and the results weren't pretty. I'd flunked.

"Well, you passed one part and failed two parts, so your total score failed overall," the instructor told me.

As I walked out and went down the elevator, I thought, *Gosh, I really am starting over. I'm serving an apprenticeship for the first time in a long time.* Apprenticeships are not all bad; you just don't want to find yourself serving in them too long.

There is a waiting period before you can take the National Futures test again. I hired a tutor, waited the required sixty days, and went in to retake the test. This time I had the flu. Once more, I was the last to finish. (A young woman from Smith Barney wrapped up at the same time.) I flunked again. At least I was consistent: finishing last and failing. This was the woman's first time to fail, and she and I walked out together after the instructor gave us the bad news.

She started to cry. I put my arm around her shoulder and tried to comfort her, saying, "It's not a big deal. We'll pass it next time." Hell, I thought, I ought to be crying too. I not only failed the test, but I was also three times her age. I reached into my pocket and pulled out one of the first business cards for my new company, BP Capital.

"Call me, and we'll give you some business," I said.

She never called. I suppose she either quit or lost her job. She missed one hell of an opportunity. She could have mentioned my name to anybody at Smith Barney, and they would have told her to call me immediately.

Going down the elevator this time I thought, *This apprenticeship is going on too long.*

Before I took the test the third time, the guys in my office said, "Boone, don't take a calculator out there. Do it like you always do. Mental arithmetic like in the office."

Mental arithmetic is second nature to me. So I went out to take the test again. This time I got there an hour early. The instructor was the same one who had told me I'd flunked on my two previous tries.

"Do you really want me to pass this test?" I asked.

"Of course I do."

"I don't think there should be a time limit. These questions are hard for me, unless they are related to the oil industry. There are a lot of currency questions, conversion to U.S. funds, and back and forth. I don't know anything about currency."

"What are you saying, Mr. Pickens?"

"Well, if I am going to take this again, I have a special request."

"Kansas City will decide that," she snapped. Then she looked up. "But what's your request?"

"That I get all day. That I can start in the morning and stay until you close."

She mulled it over for a minute. "OK, Mr. Pickens, if you don't pass the test today we'll call Kansas City and see if we can get all day on the next try."

After I turned in my test, the instructor wore a little grin.

"We don't have to call Kansas City," she said. "You passed."

Finally, I had made it. I was a licensed commodity pool operator. A geologist and a CPO both. My parents would have been so proud.

There are endless preparations and filings involved in setting up a new commodities fund. But the most important thing is fundraising. We put together a prospectus for potential investors, and I began to work the phones. First, I called my close friend and former Mesa board member John Cox, who'd always believed in me. John signed on for $10 million. Within ten years, his faith would be rewarded. His initial investment would grow to $548 million.

I called Houston investor Fayez Sarofim, who also happens to be one of the most successful money managers. I've known Fayez for forty years as both a friend and as a Mesa board member. We are the same age. "My favorite holding time is forever," Fayez likes to say.

"I'm putting in ten million dollars," I told Fayez. "Will you put in ten million as well?"

"If you're right, we're going to be great patriots by generating a lot of taxes," he said. "I'll commit to five million."

I called my longtime friend Harold Simmons. Like Cox and Sarofim, Harold was a member of the Forbes 400. I was the only one who wasn't. Good thing I had such rich friends. Harold later told me that he would have invested whatever I'd asked. I only tapped him for $5 million. He immediately said yes.

Another longtime friend and fraternity brother, Sherman Smith, a very successful drilling contractor in Tulsa, put in $3 million. Soon we had several other smaller investors, and we were up to $37 million—enough to launch BP Capital Energy Fund. We got our hands on as much technical analysis of oil and gas as we could. And we had fifty-five years in the business. Don't forget, information is everything. You can never have enough, and as you get older you find that keeping current keeps you in the game. And then there's risk. If you are going to make a lot of money, you have to take risk. Entrepreneurs put the chips on the table if they believe in their analysis. If you have 4:1 odds in your favor, and if you have the money to stay in the game long enough, you are going to win.

After a speech I made at Texas Tech University, a young man in a three-piece suit came up to me and asked, "Mr. Pickens, how will I know if I'm an entrepreneur?" I asked him what he was studying. He said he was an accounting major and was just about to take the CPA exam. I told him that I hadn't known many CPAs, lawyers, or engineers who were entrepreneurs. Then I asked him if he'd worked summers during school and what he'd done with the money he'd earned. "I've always worked, and I put it in a savings account," he said. Putting your money in a savings account is fine, but entrepreneurs, I told him, put their money at risk. Because only with risk come the greatest rewards. I suggested he invest in the stock market.

As I have often said, you can be dead right and dead if you are off thirty days in the commodities market. We were about to have a near-death experience, and the cause of it went much deeper than trading commodity futures.

IT'S FUNNY HOW sometimes the right person comes into your life at exactly the right time. John McShane is not your typical family lawyer. No matter how down I felt, McShane had been lower. For a lawyer, he's a good listener. "I know what it's like to be at rock bottom," he'd told me in our first meeting several years earlier. Twenty years before I came to see him, McShane had faced disbarment. He'd been routinely showing up drunk in court. His office phone had been cut off for nonpayment. The IRS had padlocked his office door because he hadn't paid his taxes. He'd rarely gotten home to his wife. On December 13, 1976, McShane had checked into a Dallas hotel with a stash of drugs, booze, and a pistol. He'd been determined to check out for good. Just as he'd been about to pull the trigger, he'd seen the light—an amazingly sobering moment, he calls it, when it had struck him there was a reason for him not only to live but to live at a new level. From that moment forward, he'd decided, he would commit himself to being the best lawyer, best husband, best father, best person he could be. Penniless, he faced his disbarment hearing with the only lawyer who would even consider representing him—a mentally ill attorney who would later be convicted of murder. Miraculously, on the day that lawyer represented McShane, he experienced his finest hour. McShane kept his license, redirected his life, and revived his career. He quit drinking and rebuilt his reputation as one of the best family lawyers in Texas and a warrior for good. He served on charitable boards, spearheaded initiatives for positive change, and simultaneously worked day and night for his clients.

I have always been good at picking people. I knew the minute we met in his office that day that I had found my divorce lawyer. McShane sat at his desk in the Rolex Building. He was calm and collected. I was outwardly the same, but not willing—or able—to express how I really felt. People come into McShane's office in various stages of what he calls "divorce readiness." He laid it out on his blackboard. "Look at it on a scale from one to ten," he said. "A rating of one is someone who isn't ready, who hasn't grieved the end of the marriage, who says, 'I can't believe this is happening! This is the worst day of my life! I'm not going to let this happen!' A rating of ten is, 'Where are the papers? I'm ready to sign them yesterday.'"

He sized me up. "Where are you on the scale, Boone?" he asked.

I told him that I was ready yesterday. We quickly found out that my wife was ready, too. She had already enlisted a battery of lawyers. What should have been a simple divorce petition escalated into all-out war.

Next, I told McShane what I wanted out of the divorce. A top priority was time with our dog Winston, a pedigreed papillon. I loved Winston, I told McShane. I had given the dog to her as a gift. I wanted at least visitation rights.

"OK," he said. "What else?"

The opening weekend of dove season, a near religious event for Texas hunters, was coming up in September. There was no way I was going to miss dove season at the ranch.

"OK," said McShane.

THE PEOPLE WHO followed me from Mesa believed in me. They knew me as a leader who milked every minute out of every day, a businessman of high intensity, always on full burn. As my divorce dragged on, a little bit of the guy I once was retreated to the sidelines. They tell me I didn't show the stress, that I was the same positive guy I had been before. But on some days it was a challenge to stay cool when a pack of lawyers was constantly on my heels, demanding records and threatening to depose everyone I'd ever had a conversation with. By this time every lawyer in the opposing firm was working on this case. Sometimes dozens per day.

Plus, I wasn't exactly getting quality time with Winston. During the divorce proceedings I got him every other weekend. When I first went to pick him up, old Winston started growling at me in the front seat. I think Winston had assumed I was dead, since I'd been gone from the house so long. All at once I showed up, and it spooked him. I tried the visitations on two occasions, but I decided it wasn't fair to Winston to keep picking him up and dropping him off every few weeks and having to get reacquainted each time. So for his benefit, I just stopped.

Almost every night I would have dinner with John McShane at Bob's Steak and Chop House. We would have already spent all day together, but I couldn't focus on much else. Ever see a dog chewing on a rancid bone? He's lying there gnawing away, despising what he's doing, but not willing to give up that rotten bone. That was me, chewing on my losses. I once read that four of the main triggers of depression are losing your job, moving out of your home, divorce, and the death of a family member or close friend. I was four for four. I had lost Mesa. I had moved out of my house into a hotel. My best friends, Jerry and Jane Walsh, had died in a car wreck. And my dog Winston seemed to have forgotten who I was.

I needed to move on.

McShane and I would talk beneath a reminder of my glory days hanging on the wall at Bob's: a framed cover of the December 26, 1983, issue of *Fortune*. The cover showed me in my hunting clothes with a shotgun over my shoulder. "Boone Pickens, Company

Hunter," read the cover line, referring to my takeover days. I had autographed the cover for Bob Sambol, the owner of the steak house: "Bob, a few of them got away."

McShane would have to sit next to my good ear so I could hear him over the roar of the dining room. I was living alone for the first time in a long time. Since I didn't cook, I'd ask the waitress to pack up half of my steak to take home. After hours of replaying the sordid events of the day, I would leave the steak house with my doggy bag as the lawsuit dragged on and on, diverting my attention from my new business when it needed my attention the most.

CHAPTER 4

The Bottom of the Canyon

Booneism #10: Show me a good loser, and I'll show you a loser.

"WE COMMENCED TRADING on June 24," I wrote in our first monthly investors' letter, which was dated July 11, 1997. "We did show a degree of patience before we made our first move. We are starting to build our fall and winter positions as we get comfortable with the fundamentals."

My trading philosophy? Keep things simple.

Anything and everything seems to affect the price of oil and natural gas. I rely on continuous information flow. Weather, war, politics, the economy—you get the picture. True to our roots, the BP Capital Energy Fund invested exclusively in energy futures, either long, believing that the price was going to rise, or short, believing that the price was going to fall. There are times when we're long both oil and gas, or short both of these commodities. At other times we may be long one and short the other.

I don't invest on hunches. We are not day traders. Our investments are based on fundamentals: our analysis of the forces of supply and demand. It is a lot simpler than some might think. It is also, surprisingly, not the norm in commodities trading, where peaks and valleys trigger buy and sell orders that "technical" or "black box" traders follow.

It amazes me that a trader would invest money based on what a computer tells him or her to do instead of relying on research to predict price movement. Those who trade on technical analysis frequently succumb to a pack mentality because their actions are computer-driven or chart-driven, instead of the result of knowledge and experience.

Let me give you an example: If the price of oil drops to $80 a barrel, the computer triggers a buy signal. If the price rises to $120, the computer triggers a sell signal. Don't get the idea that I ignore technical information. I don't. Still, there are other factors to consider, such as an economy headed into a recession, a weak housing market, a war in the Middle East, a tough winter freeze—or the fact that we've peaked on oil production globally.

Some people make a living day trading, but it's a business I don't understand. There is money to be made by technical trading, which is why I invest with my good friend Salem Abraham, a very successful technical trader.

To make the big money, I've found it's best to take a long-term view, stay focused, and not get spooked by the temporary fluctuations in the market. When I have the odds in my favor, I put my money up and keep it up. If the fundamentals change, I get the hell out of there.

For example, we may own 1,000 contracts of May crude at $93. Each contract is 1,000 barrels of oil. Fast-forward a month. If the price of oil is up to $100, we made $7 a barrel. On the 1,000 contracts, you make a paper profit of $7 million. Again, the big money is usually in the long term. The most important thing is to stay with your position. Many traders see oil go up a dollar or so, and they take the profit and go to the tall grass. They just don't feel the risk is worth it. But if the fundamentals are in place and as you gain confidence, you might even add more contracts.

I've been doing this long enough to know that about the time you panic, you're going to lose. One of my guys coined a phrase for the way I'll stay with a position. He calls it "hanging on to the tub"—the most important thing is to focus and to stay cool.

Back in 1997, I was preoccupied. And a loser. The performance of the BP Capital Energy Fund mirrored my sinking spirits. McShane likes to say that if we had charted my mood along with the fund's performance, both graphs would have shown the same downhill slide.

My letters to investors during this period reflect exactly that:

August 12, 1997: The Fund's net loss for July 1–31 was $1,403,521.14.

September 12, 1997: The Fund's net loss for the month of August was $5,058,546.14.

October 14, 1997: The Fund's net gain for the month of September was $1,705,095.50.

November 14, 1997: The Fund's net loss for the month of October was $1,097,769.42.

December 18, 1997: The Fund's net loss for the month of November was $13,311,080.56.

We had been trading ten straight years, and these were my first losses. I could have stood them a lot better at Mesa than I could on my own. Throughout my career, I've been known for my optimism and belief that any obstacles or failures could be overcome. Now everything seemed to be going downhill. The company wasn't doing well. I wasn't doing well. *Where are we headed?* I would think throughout the night.

McShane and I were almost two years into the divorce proceeding, and it had consumed us both. Like two soldiers in a foxhole, we'd been constantly under fire side by side. McShane had become my friend and confidant as well as my lawyer. He was deeply dedicated to me and my case and was one of those emotional and affectionate Irish types who wasn't afraid to hug people and tell them he loved them. By then he was having heart problems. So he stuck to a strict diet and tried to remain calm, which wasn't easy.

The stress of helping me with my divorce had also taken a heavy toll on my longtime associate Ron Bassett, who was wearing a cast for a stress fracture on his leg. He also appeared to be suffering from exhaustion. We were like the walking wounded, physically and mentally.

"It doesn't look like we are going into battle but coming back from one," I cracked as we all limped toward the courtroom for another torturous hearing.

"You ought to look at yourself," McShane told me.

He could see me as I couldn't. At sixty-nine, I had spent most of my life winning. Now I was taking some hard hits. From the way our investments were going, it also appeared I had some challenges there, too. I was up to my ass in alligators.

Booneism #11: *I told a friend, "This is the kind of market that builds character." He looked at me and said, "If it gets any worse, you'll have more character than Abe Lincoln."*

GREG SHUTTLESWORTH CAME to see me in 1998. Greg is executive director of natural gas for Petroleum Industry Research Associates Energy Group (PIRA). PIRA is a leading consulting firm, and Greg is their natural gas expert. He had worked for David Rockefeller in the Energy Group at Chase Bank. Greg was only twenty-six when he became the author of an energy report for Chase called *The Petroleum Situation.* After working with Chase, he joined Gary Ross at PIRA.

Greg is intense, passionate, and stubborn. He is paid to give the cold, hard facts, supported by charts and slides and delivered with passion. There are no gray areas with Greg; he always believes he is right, and back then he was bearish. His unwavering pessimism about the industry so offended the major producers that they would call his boss and threaten to terminate PIRA's services. Greg was undaunted.

"Every producer is bullish," he says. "Why drill for something when the price is going down? My instinct is to be bearish. When prices go up, people who produce goods—whether shoes or cars or oil and gas—make more, inflate supplies, and push prices down. Producers always shoot themselves in the foot. As soon as they get a price they like, they bring new production on the market, and the price goes in the tank."

Greg had been bearish on the natural gas market for some time. I first met Greg and Gary when they came to see us at Mesa in the summer of 1986. Back then, I was extremely bullish on natural gas. Greg came into our office and insisted that the price wasn't going to rise, not back then, maybe never. "Where were you when I needed you?" I asked Greg during this first visit to BP Capital.

When he came to see us in the spring of 1998, we were long natural gas. Greg was set on convincing us that the gas market was going into oversupply and we needed to reverse our position. He had been spreading this news all week on the road, which typically involved meetings with three or four oil company executives every day in Houston, Dallas, Tulsa, and elsewhere. Sometimes he would conduct eighteen briefings a week, giving the same report over and over.

Some business leaders make the mistake of tuning out opposing opinions and potential bad news. I believe in gathering as much information as possible: good, bad, and everything in between. Let the hide come with the hair is how I look at it. The more we know, the better informed our decisions will be—at least that was how it was supposed to work.

In the United States, natural gas generates 22 percent of all electricity and 60 percent of all home heating. It is also a critical resource in the manufacture of fertilizer. Like oil, there is not an infinite supply of natural gas, but it is the second largest fossil fuel resource in the United States, second only to coal. Greg was bearish at this point. He saw more gas coming on the market, which meant lower prices ahead. "I wouldn't want to be bullish," Greg said.

We were on the opposite side of the fence, holding a long position on natural gas in the belief that prices were going to rise in the winter of 1998 based on our analysis that demand would exceed supply.

Determined to convince us that he was right, Greg came in with a full presentation. He was, as always, intense, extremely serious, and forceful. He talked about how the recent deregulation would lead to oversupply and reduced demand. The conversation then turned to deepwater drilling in the Gulf of Mexico, which Greg was convinced would lead to significant supply growth.

There was considerable information about new production from deep water in the Gulf, and Greg had bought into this hype. I was never convinced of the deepwater potential. We believed production would come online more slowly and turn out to be far less than the hype suggested. I still believed that demand would eventually outstrip supply—and that natural gas prices would increase.

By the end of 1997, most major oil companies considered the deep water to be a prime target for exploration and development. It was their last kiss at the pig. In the past, reserves equivalent to 100 million barrels of oil had been the minimum required to make such deepwater projects economical. Now technology had lowered exploration costs and increased the alternatives for offshore deepwater facilities. As a result, deepwater projects that previously would not have made sense were becoming more attractive.

Operators in the Gulf of Mexico were supposedly encountering flow rates that rivaled those in the North Sea or the Middle East. The deep water "will be the principal area of growth for us for the remainder of this century," Shell Exploration & Production president Jack Little said in early 1997. At the Twenty-ninth Offshore Technology Conference in Houston in May 1997, Rich Pattarozzi, president and CEO of Shell Deepwater Development, said, "The opportunity that we have in deep water is huge, not only in the Gulf of Mexico but around the world."

I didn't agree with them. I thought that the deepwater explo-
rationists had the Big Eye Syndrome. What they found would only
be a fraction of what they thought it would be.

Greg Shuttlesworth had been infected by the Big Eye Syndrome
on the deepwater production, too. He and I disagreed on the potential, although we agreed that production in shallower water along
the continental shelf would continue to decline. Natural gas was
not falling as fast as crude oil prices back then, but the drop in both
was affecting drilling activity. The impact was not so much on the
deepwater projects run by the major oil and gas companies as on
the smaller shallow-water operators on the outer continental shelf.
The question was, *How fast and how steep would the decline in
production be?*

Greg went on and on, saying that the increase from deepwater
production in 1998 to 1999 would make the shallow-water decline
a moot point. If the predictions of major producers turned out to
be right, the deep water would come fast, increasing supply and
forcing prices down.

I sat around the table in my office with Ron and Mike Larson,
who had replaced Bob Kultgen, and we all listened to Greg's pitch.
He pounded his marker on a presentation board, scribbling facts
and figures and insisting that anyone who was bullish on price
was going to get his dress over his head. In our opposing view,
we maintained that supply and demand and weather expectations
for the winter of 1998 had convinced us that we were right in our
long bet.

"Who have you been talking to?" I asked Greg.

"Shell, Vastar, Dominion, Amoco, and BP," he said, mentioning the
big gas producers, who were all aggressively promoting deep water
as a prime supply site.

In March 1998, for example, Shell announced plans to expand its production in the Gulf of Mexico by developing three new deepwater discoveries, according to the *Oil and Gas Journal*. The projects were expected to "increase to 14 the number of deepwater developments in which Shell has an interest." Their daily production from these new projects was expected to reach 135,000 barrels of oil and 170 million cubic feet of natural gas per day.

We went back and forth. Greg assured us that increased deepwater production and high storage capacity would result in an oversupply and drive prices down so that we should be short natural gas. We advocated maintaining our long position, because we believed that the forecasts for high storage levels were being driven by industry hype. Industry sources were forecasting that deepwater production would reach 8 billion cubic feet or more. I didn't see it happening.

Greg was extremely convincing, and I didn't have intensity to my position. I was really down mentally. In addition, we had been losing money on our long positions. In the end, we took Greg's advice. We began unwinding our long natural gas contracts and going short, betting on the oversupply scenario that would cause prices to drop. I was going against my own instincts and the fundamentals that I had built my career upon. It was a costly mistake.

The deepwater production in the gulf did not meet expectations, and storage levels were lower than expected. Prices rose instead of falling. Things would only get worse. In 1999, deep water produced 2.4 billion cubic feet of natural gas a day. In 2000 that number was up to only 2.8 billion cubic feet, when analysts had been predicting 3.5. It was slower to get going than the major producers had expected, because there were a lot more problems associated with the deepwater projects. Shell, being the biggest producer of them all, was not willing to let on that production was slipping. On top of that, shallow-water production in the gulf was declining faster also. From 1999 to 2000, it dropped from 12.5 billion cubic feet a day to 11.7. Today production has fallen all the way to 5 billion cubic feet a day.

We started May 1998 with $13 million in the BP Capital Energy Fund. In just one year we were down $24 million, and it was only going to get worse. By January 1999 we had ridden it down to just $2.7 million. In ten years' trading at Mesa, I had never had a run like this. "This is about as bad as it can get," I wrote in a letter to our investors. I was now scratching a poor man's ass.

Also at this time, my close friend and longtime ally John Cox had a massive stroke while undergoing a procedure for a clogged carotid artery. Each month after that, I made a point of visiting John in Midland. He always knew me and smiled, and we would both cry.

Ron Bassett had been talking to John several months before his stroke.

"We're really struggling," Ron told him. "We can't get anything to work."

The $10 million John had invested in our fund was down by 90 percent. Still, he never doubted us for a second.

"Don't worry," John said. "Boone will pull us out."

A framed picture of John, with a plaque bearing that quote, hangs in our office to this day.

Booneism #12: When you blow away the foam, you get down to the real stuff.

THERE WAS A reason we weren't firing on all cylinders. I was suffering from undiagnosed depression. Entrepreneurs, in particular, tend to develop a sense of infallibility. Often they neglect their personal lives and their mental health. They don't allow themselves time to relax or recharge. They don't work out or watch what they eat. Physical and mental health problems bring you down just as easily as other factors, and I had clearly let something slip.

Greg Shuttlesworth was a smart guy, and he was right far more than he was wrong, but this time he was wrong. Every leader makes a bad call now and then. You've got to take the hit, learn from it, come up with a new plan, and move on. We paid a big price—our fund was down more than 90 percent. Did you hear that? We were close to being out of business.

A couple of investors bailed on us. I couldn't blame them. They didn't understand the losses, and I'm not sure I did either. Most of our investors stayed the course. My friend Harold Simmons, whose $5 million had been reduced to $400,000, never even called to complain.

Ron Bassett said, "If oil goes to $400 a barrel, we've got this thing whipped."

"Stay level. It's going to get better. It always gets better," I told my group as we sat in the bullpen with our desks jammed together, eating our lunch of take-out sandwiches.

"I've never lost so much money at a critical time in my life," I told Gary Ross.

Our new company was facing a real gut check—or worse. If we were wrong again, we might just have to fold our tent. Yet somehow I felt that we weren't finished. I felt that there was something more and that we would be OK.

"We're going to come back," I kept telling Ron and Mike in our daily meetings. We had stopped taking management fees, and I didn't intend to charge fees until the fund got back in the black, which is unusual in the investment business. That was not the first time I had waived income. Back at Mesa in the really down days, I didn't take a salary when the shareholders weren't receiving dividends in 1990 and 1991. Now, at BP, we would be down to trading as few as twenty contracts. I didn't let on, but my legendary optimism was being sorely tested—or at least something was. It was John McShane who convinced me I was clinically depressed.

McShane knew a thing or two about depression; he'd experienced it himself. He knew the signs, and he saw them in me: sleep deprivation, fatigue, lethargy, irritability, loss of focus.

"I want you to see somebody," he told me.

I had ratcheted down into depression for a decade and never realized what was happening. Now I had hit bottom. A psychiatrist put me on antidepressants. It turned out to be a quick fix. Everything started clearing up. The things I felt I couldn't change began to change. I felt better, exercised more, and was soon back to being Boone again. I began emerging from a really dark decade. Everything was starting to fall into place. I realize it's not that easy for everybody, but I was fortunate.

Looking back on my past, things began to make sense. It wasn't the world against Boone. It was Boone against Boone. Once I put the past behind me, my mind cleared, my focus returned, and I was on my way.

Things will get better if you hang in there and believe in yourself. The attributes and skills that made you successful in the first place don't disappear. I had been struggling at the plate, but I was entering a period when nearly every swing would hit the ball out of the park.

As always, success hinged on the price of oil and gas. After a decade of being too early, my theories were finally about to be proven right. It wasn't enough to merely be ready for the challenge mentally. I also had to be prepared physically. And I had a plan for that.

> **Booneism #13:** *When you're young, fitness is a sport. As you grow older, it's a necessity.*

AS MY MIND cleared and my focus returned, I stepped up my commitment to physical fitness. No amount of money, success, or fame can raise a body from a bed or turn fat into muscle. My friend Arnold Schwarzenegger has said that weights in a gym never care about how rich or famous you are. Only constant and aggressive exercise can keep a human being young and fit.

When I was thirty, I didn't have much time for exercise. Yes, I always loved basketball and played in pickup games in my twenties. Then I dropped out for a few years until I was introduced to racquetball. A high school friend, Jack Fuqua, invited me to play him in a game. I'd never played racquetball before. Being athletic and confident, I thought I could beat Jack. I was wrong. Racquetball is an intense cardiovascular workout, especially if you are not in shape. By the end of the game I was so worn out that I had to lie down on a bench to rest.

"This is exactly why I called you," Fuqua told me. "You're not doing anything to take care of yourself. The only exercise you get is playing golf or bird hunting."

That racquetball game changed my life. I stepped up my commitment to fitness and began playing racquetball at the YMCA on a regular basis. After a year, I called Jack for a rematch and beat him.

After I took up racquetball and then jogging, I noticed a big difference in how I felt. My stamina improved. So did my powers of concentration. I got a lot more done and had energy to spare. Exercise did so much for me that I was sure it would have the same effect for our company. We bought everyone at Mesa memberships at the YMCA, but there was a catch. They had to use it, or I'd take it back. In 1979, we built a $2.5 million fitness center on the third floor of our parking garage. It had four racquetball courts, a full basketball court, an indoor running track, and state-of-the-art exercise equipment. I'm convinced it was the most complete corporate fitness center anywhere.

Mesa became among the first companies in America to institute a corporate wellness program, and within three years our wellness center paid for itself in health-care savings. Our company's per-employee health-care cost dropped almost 60 percent below the national average. The average number of sick days for those enrolled in the program also dropped dramatically. Mesa gave cash incentives to employees if their families participated in the fitness program. A ten-year study on annual medical claims from 1980 through 1989 found that the average annual medical costs of wellness program participants were one-half those of the company's nonparticipants. I couldn't get everybody on board, but I got most of them. The only way all of this works is if the CEO is a serious participant, and I was as serious as a heart attack on this subject.

In 1985, Mesa was named the Most Physically Fit Company in America by the President's Council on Physical Fitness. We competed for the title against corporate giants in a competition held in Houston. During the event, I went down to check on my team.

"Do you know where the Mesa camp is?" I asked a woman who was dripping in sweat after just finishing a competition.

"No, I don't," she said, "but wherever they are, I'm sure they're gloating over another gold medal." Just what I wanted to hear.

"EXERCISE DOES MORE than build muscles and help prevent heart disease. New science shows that it also boosts brainpower and may offer hope in the battle against Alzheimer's," was the sub-head of a recent *Newsweek* cover story called "Exercise and the Brain." I also believe it builds your self-confidence.

I never abandoned fitness as a priority. I don't want to be taken out of the game because I didn't take care of myself. But during my depression, I lost focus in my fitness program. I was still working out, but not with the determination and discipline that a man entering his seventies requires. That was about to change.

"Do you want to work out as hard as you can?" my trainer Eric Oberg asked when we began our daily workouts.

"Push me to the limit," I said, and we were on our way. Eric has become a very important member of our staff, keeping me alive and ensuring that our bodies keep pace with our brains. I began working with Eric in 1992. He not only trains me but he's also come on full-time at BP Capital and is available to work with any-one on the staff. We built an in-house gym at BP Capital, and it's the first or last stop for many of us each day. I usually start my day in sweats and running shoes by 6:30 a.m. Eric has a mandate to push me hard and keep me strong. He got his fitness training certifica-tion at the nationally recognized Cooper Clinic, where Ken Cooper coined the term *aerobics* in 1968.

By the time I start my workout, our two traders—Michael Ross and David Meaney—are already at their desks. I get the morning reports from them first and then go into my workout routine. It's simple and straightforward and rigorous. The more you push your-self, the better the results.

Here's how our workouts typically go:

- Cardio: Eric sets the treadmill for fifteen to twenty minutes at 4 miles an hour at an 8- to 12-degree grade. Periodically, we will do sprints, and I'll run until I've upped my heart rate to 140. As Eric likes to say, "It's an ass kicker."

- Weights: From one day to the next, my exercise routine feels either easy or hard. On the days when the weights feel heav-ier than normal, we back off the intensity a bit. On the days when everything feels good—which, luckily, is most days—we push hard.

- Some days we work the chest: four sets of eight to twelve rep-etitions, with the understanding that each set is always done until failure—meaning I lift until I can't do another rep. At that point Eric typically asks me to do one more, and I push past that tough spot toward greater success.

- The next day we'll focus on arms or back and shoulders. For arms we do dips, feet on one bench, sitting on an opposite bench, and lowering your body between the benches using just your arms. We'll do curls with 35-pound dumbbells in each hand. For back, I'll do many different variations on pull-ups.

- Next day, we'll focus on leg strength. We start off with three to four sets of squats, using 40-pound dumbbells in each hand. These are followed by three sets of fifty walking lunges, with a 40-pound weighted vest on.

- Every other day, we will do abdominal crunches: twenty crunches per set, two or three sets, with a 15-pound dumbbell on my chest. I never forget the words of Arnold Schwarzenegger: "The last three or four reps of each set are what make the muscle grow. This area of pain divides the champion from someone else who is not a champion. That's what most people lack, having the guts to go on and just say they'll go through the pain no matter what happens." I speak with Governor Schwarzenegger occasionally, and one of these days I'm going to invite him to work out with me.

Fitness competitions are something we like. Not long ago, we challenged Clean Energy Fuels, the company we created to advance natural gas as a transportation fuel, to a fitness competition. The more involvement, the better for everyone. We use the Cooper Clinic treadmill stress test as our model. The team with the highest average times wins, and the winner presents the other team with the Losers Cup.

I like to compete against Eric on the treadmill at our annual physicals at the Cooper Clinic. Three years ago, I beat him. In the last two years, Eric beat me, outlasting me by three seconds the first year and one second the next. Eric is forty-four.

Fitness is a daily priority. Several years ago, *Time,* in its famous "Ten Questions" piece, asked whether I considered myself a fitness fanatic. "No," I answered, noting that "last year I worked out an average of 24.4 days a month." Fanatic? Maybe.

I'm convinced that workouts strengthen not only my body but also my mind. I never feel overwhelmed, and I rarely feel tired despite one of the toughest business schedules I've ever had. "I've been working for you for twenty-five years, and you're in better physical condition today than you were when I started," Sally Geymüller told me recently.

At my last annual physical at the Cooper Clinic, I lasted longer on the treadmill than I did twenty-two years earlier. As I like to tell Eric, I work out so that when I'm old I can still do whatever I want. Eric laughs at the part about "when" I'm old. As I've said before, age is just a number. This was true when I was seventy and is even more so today.

CHAPTER 5

Loading the Boat

Booneism #14: *"Do you just like to get your back to the wall to see if you can get off?" No, but I play good off the wall.*

IN EARLY 2000, Greg Shuttlesworth came back to see us again. This time something was very different. Greg unpacked his briefcases for his presentation as Ron Bassett, Mike Larson, and I sat around the conference table in my office. My dog Murdock wandered in and out. The price of natural gas at that time was still struggling in the $2 to $2.50 range.

"What do you think about three-dollar gas this summer?" I asked Greg.

Instead of his typical bearish reply, he was actually . . . *bullish*.

"That's not only a slam dunk, we'll probably see twice that price," he said.

To hear an old bear like Greg support our bullish position was exciting even to Murdock. As soon as Greg started delivering his sunny scenario, Murdock ran into the room and jumped on Greg's lap, where he remained during the entire presentation. Greg said supply would soon drop while demand would skyrocket. Electric power companies had shifted to natural gas for power generation, and the simple dynamics of supply not keeping pace with demand would drive the price up. This time the increase in natural gas prices would not be slow, as it had been in the 1990s. Instead late 2000 would mark the biggest rise in the history of natural gas.

We were on the same page as Greg.

"We're gonna load the boat," I said.

"You should get another boat and fill that, too," Greg said.

What I had been predicting since the early 1990s, when I'd effectively bet Mesa on the belief that natural gas prices would rise, was finally about to happen.

Remember, the price of natural gas was $2.20 at the beginning of 2000. By early November the price was around $4.50, igniting an explosive rally and one hell of a month. It was the perfect storm: decreased supply plus rising demand equaled higher prices, in this case through the roof. By late December 2000, the price of natural gas had risen to a new historic high of $10.10. We had loaded the boat and gone long natural gas. For the year 2000, the BP Capital Energy Fund was up $252 million, a gain of 9,095 percent before fees. We distributed $222 million to our investors. They couldn't believe it. I couldn't believe it. It was a sweet reward for those who had hung in there with us.

At the end of that year, I sensed a shift ahead. Natural gas inventories were building, and $10 natural gas was destroying demand. We reversed course, taking our position from long to short just as the upward curve peaked and headed south. By the last trading day in 2000, prices had fallen to $9.42. In the new year, the bulls thought they could regain their footing and brought the market back up to $9.87. The rally failed to attract new buying interest, and the slippery slope turned into an avalanche. By March 2001 prices had slid to almost $5, and by September 2001 they were all the way back to where they had started the upward move, at around $2.20. BP Capital had begun what one industry observer described in *Fortune* as "one of the great individual trading runs of all time."

We finally had a good news story to tell. Looking for other ideas and investments, we decided to launch a second fund, the BP Capital Energy Equity Fund, in 2001. We wanted to take advantage of our analysis on the oil and gas commodities and apply it to the stock market, specializing in energy and energy-dependent stocks. It was a page from my old playbook. We would identify under-performing energy companies and take sizable positions in them. Then we would urge the company's executives to take actions to improve their stock price and become more stockholder friendly. If that didn't happen, we would push for a sale or a merger. Either way, we would stand to make a nice profit. I wasn't looking to go hostile. I'd had all I wanted of that business.

In mid-2001, we hit the road to look for investors.

We went to New York to see my old friend Ace Greenberg, chairman of Bear Sterns. "You guys will be about as welcome as malaria," Ace told us after we had explained the concept to him in his office. Next we went to Houston to see my friend and original commodities fund investor Fayez Sarofim.

"Why do you want to do something like that?" Fayez said when we told him our plans for the equity fund. "Your commodity fund is working fine. Why do you want to mess with all of this other stuff?"

"This won't work if you can't raise a billion dollars," Harold Simmons told me, and he suggested we hire an investment banker to raise the money.

It was not the most rousing reception for our new equity fund, but they all eventually invested. Harold Simmons put in his money with the stipulation that if the fund sank to a certain level, he could bail. Fayez and the family of my old friend John Cox anted up. We had $84 million committed. We felt we needed more, so we enlisted a fund-raiser to introduce us to the people who ran some of the biggest pension and endowment funds, including the ones at Stanford University and Cambridge Associates in Boston, as well as some individual investors. We also met with CalPERS, the California Public Employees' Retirement System. CalPERS is the biggest pension fund in the United States, with an estimated $250 billion under management.

We made pitch books, then went to meet with the pension fund executives. My attorney Bobby Stillwell was our wise old head. Garrett Smith was back on our team from the Mesa days, when he'd been a financial analyst. Now he was the numbers-and-details guy. And I was the seasoned veteran of the oil and gas business. After fifty-five years, you'd think so. I spoke first, discussing my half century in the oil business, my successes at Mesa, in both exploration and during the takeover era.

"Well, with all due respect, you really don't have a track record" was the standard reply. I was taken aback. The way I saw it, I had a lengthy track record. I told them about the BP Capital Energy Fund and the recent success that we had enjoyed. Then we got down to the meat of the matter: how the equity fund was a natural extension of our commodity analysis.

"What we mean, Mr. Pickens, is you don't have a track record of managing an equity fund," they said. "You have to have at least a three-year record."

Bobby Stillwell looked at me and I looked at Garrett. Finally, I said, "I'm the hardest-working man on the planet." I explained about getting up early, about working out regularly, about staying young, about watching the market like a hawk.

"How do you think it went?" I asked our advisor after the meeting.

"It went fine," he said, "but you're not going to get any money."

The pension funds passed on investing with us at least at this time. At seventy-four, my age was a factor. Some were confused about how to categorize our fund. They didn't have an easily explainable "box" to put us in. Others were never interested in investing, they admitted afterward; they just wanted to meet me because of my past record. I was an oddity, but not near as much of an oddity as I was a couple of years later.

Still, we moved forward. With $84 million from our investors, the BP Capital Energy Equity Fund was launched on August 1, 2001. One month and ten days later came the attack on the World Trade Center. The stock market was closed for six days. When it opened again, the Dow had dropped 684 points. Once again, oil and gas prices nosedived. Thank God we had not made any investments at that point.

The first companies we targeted were Penn Virginia and Vintage Petroleum. If you buy more than 5 percent of a company's stock, and your intentions are other than passive, the SEC requires you to disclose it in what's called a 13D filing. So we filed on both Penn Virginia (acquiring 7.1 percent) and Vintage Petroleum (8.4 percent). We ultimately made an offer to acquire Penn Virginia. They said, "Forget it." They wanted no part of our ideas. Then we made a proposal to Vintage, outlining ways that they could restructure their company and add value. Both of these offers were friendly, not hostile. Ace had been right. We were about as welcome as malaria.

We went to Tulsa and met with Vintage's CEO and chairman. Once we arrived, we were hurried into a conference room. "I don't like what you're doing," he told us. It was obvious we weren't going to get anywhere with these guys.

In 2001, the Teacher Retirement System of Texas (TRS) made a $25 million investment in the fund. By the end of the year, after we had bought stock in companies that were sold before we were able to disclose our holdings, our equity fund was up 18 percent. We were smart enough to know that we had lucked into these breaks. The concept was unproven. I was starting to question our business plan.

By mid-2002 the equity fund was down nearly 40 percent. Both Penn Virginia's and Vintage's stock prices had declined. The managements weren't maximizing the potential of their assets. The market was not convinced we were going to influence any management. In late 2002, we knew for sure we had a flawed strategy. We were trying to play on our 1980s reputation, and it didn't work. The missing link was the fact that we didn't have enough money. Harold Simmons's advice—that our equity fund wouldn't work unless we could raise $1 billion—turned out to be correct. Our original plan hadn't worked, so we began retooling our strategy.

The Teacher Retirement System, which had made a $25 million investment in the fund, wanted out and was taken out with a small profit, which would have grown to $193 million if it had stayed in.

I was a guest of Harold Simmons at his home in Santa Barbara in September 2002, and he asked when I was going to get our equity fund "up and going." I told him I was as disappointed as he was. He was still not convinced the equity fund was a good idea. "If I could switch some of the money over and play the natural gas commodity, we have a great opportunity coming up fast," I told Harold. He asked how much money I wanted to allocate to commodities. I said $10 million. "Ah, hell, make the play and get it on its feet," Harold said. At that point, $10 million was a big investment for the fund. When gas spiked up in the winter of 2002–03, our $10 million investment in the natural gas play made $125 million. The equity fund made back all of its losses and was in the black. It recovered our 2002 losses and left us with a good year in 2003. I called Harold and told him, "We're up and going now."

We converted the fund into a passive investment vehicle, which means there would be no attempts at takeovers and no 13D positions in underperforming oil and gas companies. The BP Capital Energy Equity Fund became what it is today: an investment vehicle with a blend of futures (10 percent) and energy stocks (90 percent). We would go both long and short. At the close of 2007, the BP Capital Energy Equity Fund was up 1,140 percent before fees since its inception. It is a hedge fund; per SEC requirements, in order to purchase a percentage ownership in a limited partnership, one must be a sophisticated investor and have $5 million in investments, a net worth of more than $1.5 million, and the ability to sustain the loss of his or her entire stake in the fund. The investors pay a monthly management fee equal to one-twelfth of 1.75 percent of the beginning monthly value of their investments, as well as 20 percent of their annual profits to us as a performance incentive fee.

Meanwhile, the BP Capital Energy Fund took a $98 million loss in October 2001 after being up $211 million through September of that year. Other traders were going bust all around us that fall, all related to the collapse of Enron, as well as 9/11. It was a period of great uncertainty, and it was taking a toll on the industry. We finished 2001 up $147 million in the commodity fund. It was rough going in the first half of 2002, and we found ourselves down nearly 48 percent by midsummer.

By August 2002, the natural gas price was $3.50 three to five years out. I was convinced that the price was going up. We had to figure out a way to get more natural gas exposure. The fund was strapped for cash. So we had to get creative—*quick.*

Michael Ross is our chief commodities trader. When I met him in the summer of 2001 he was twenty-five and had been working for his father, Gary Ross, the head of PIRA. Before that, he'd worked for Marcstone Capital, the foreign currency and European equity fund. I was in PIRA's New York offices when Gary brought his son in to meet me. I've always prided myself in the ability to spot talent. I had a sense about Michael. He seemed aggressive, extremely smart, and unhappy in his present position.

"You know, your son is not very happy," I told Gary.

"Oh, hell, he'll be all right."

"Well, it doesn't look like he enjoys what he's doing. Why don't I take him to Dallas and see if he can do some good with me?"

Michael, who had never been to Texas, said sure, he'd like to check it out. He flew down in the morning and left that afternoon. He told me later that he'd read my book, *Boone,* on the plane. He knew I'd be more fun to work for than his dad. When he landed back in New York, he called me and said he was interested in the job.

"How much would it take to get you down here?" I asked him.

"A hundred grand or so, but I'll trade," he said, meaning he was flexible.

"I'll give you sixty-two."

"Done," said Michael.

He flew back and moved into an apartment he had leased

online. The next morning he was at his desk, staring at a single screen, which quickly grew into several, in an otherwise empty office, and was off and running, talking a mile a minute.

Michael runs in one gear—overdrive. Every morning he is in his office before dawn, staring at an array of computer screens showing the commodities markets, the weather, world news events— anything and everything that can affect our business. And throughout the day and night he is in constant contact with me. He's extremely energetic, to say the least.

In August 2002, we had around five thousand crude contracts and eight thousand natural gas contracts. About half of them expired within a year, and the other half expired further out. Michael was scanning weather reports throughout the day and night, paying particular attention to pressure gradients, water vapor maps, actual readings taken from planes, and on and on. So much information it'll wear you out.

In addition to gathering information, Michael has the responsibility of presenting all of the trading ideas he hears from our brokers. One day, Michael came barreling into my office with a new idea. He had been presented a "three-way" strategy that excited him. We were stretched pretty thin at that point. I was determined to stay safe. This three-way was a strategy of calls and puts, which enabled us to get additional exposure on natural gas with very little initial capital. It was the perfect play for us at that time, since we were low on cash.

We bought natural gas to expire in 2003, 2004, and 2005, putting on what we call the "4-5-3": buying a $4 call, selling a $5 call, and selling a $3 put. It boils down to a strategy that produces a profit window from $4 to $5 with no risk, unless gas goes below $3. Gas was at $3.50. We felt that for the three years ahead, natural gas prices would exceed $4 but wouldn't go lower than $3. This "three-way" was a zero cost, but we had to make margin calls if it moved against us. It was a cinch. "They're giving it to us," I told my guys. "We can't turn it down."

> ***Booneism #15:*** *Be willing to make decisions. That's the most important quality in a good leader. Don't fall victim to what I call the "ready-aim-aim-aim-aim" syndrome. You must be willing to fire.*

WE BEGAN MAKING money on our three-ways. I was convinced that we were going to run short of gas by the summer of 2003. That, of course, meant higher prices. I was so convinced that I was willing to bet big. The fundamentals were aligned. In the winter, the industry draws gas from storage to meet winter demand. Starting in late spring through early fall, you should fill storage. We were convinced that the production wasn't enough to fill to capacity for the next winter.

Natural gas is a domestic commodity, as opposed to oil, which is a global product, with the United States being the largest importer. And while the price of oil is dependent on many factors, the price of natural gas is tied mostly to the weather. Natural gas is stored in underground facilities at strategic places across the United States. But it is priced from NYMEX trading at Henry Hub, "America's natural gas energy portal," which is a nexus of natural gas pipeline systems near the town of Erath, Louisiana.

You're at capacity once storage reaches 3.2 trillion cubic feet, a figure that has since been increased to 3.6 trillion cubic feet. If consumers need more during the winter, it can be supplied only from production, storage, and a small amount of imported liquefied natural gas (LNG). When you get in this spot, it means the price is going to go up.

I felt certain that natural gas production was going to be disappointing because of lower prices and declining reserves. When the price is down, there is less drilling, which means that at some point production will be lower. This can quickly drive prices higher, which spurs drilling.

That's exactly what had been happening in 2001 and 2002. Prices were extremely low. After the 9/11 attacks, America's economy was reeling. Commodity prices were down almost across the board. Everything was pointing to prices impacting production, and once production came down, prices had to go back up.

We figured one winter with below-normal temperatures, and natural gas would take off like a scalded dog. Again, supply and demand. Winter was right around the corner, and we were feeling very bullish.

Our three-way option strategy was starting to look like a bases-loaded home run. We started buying gas futures outright. We were so confident that the price was going to rise that we continued to build a major position. We were buying seven-month strips—500 contracts per month—3,500 contracts at a time. Each of those strips represented $140 million worth of natural gas at $4. We were headed into autumn, which can be a risky time to be long natural gas. It's known as the shoulder season, because there is usually no weather-driven demand for natural gas; it's neither too hot nor too cold. Autumn can make the market feel weak, and often prices trade off during this time. So we were taking a risk being long into the shoulder, especially with this much size.

Since the biggest and most important force that moves the natural gas market up or down is weather, trading natural gas futures is extremely volatile. You can have everything right, and weather can make or break the play. It's like when people say the three most important things in real estate are "location, location, location." In natural gas, it's "weather, weather, weather."

On September 25, 2002, a series of unusual events took place. Tropical Storm Isidore hit the Gulf of Mexico, followed by Hurricane Lili on October 3. Neither was as powerful a storm as we would see a few years later, but their "one-two punch," as it can be described, was enough to cause havoc.

GULF STORMS SHUT DOWN U.S. OFFSHORE OIL
AND NATURAL GAS PRODUCTION

Nearly 10 million barrels of oil and 60 billion cubic feet of natural gas have been unavailable for U.S. consumption because of the shutdown of oil and gas operations on the Gulf of Mexico outer continental shelf due to the effects of Tropical Storm Isidore and Hurricane Lili.

Last week, reports to the Minerals Management Service by the oil and gas industry in the Gulf indicated that about 95 percent of crude oil and 60 percent of natural gas production were shut down from Wednesday, September 25, 2002, through Friday, September 27, 2002, as a result of Tropical Storm Isidore. As production was being returned over the weekend, the threat of Hurricane Lili curtailed the full resumption of production. On Monday, September 30, 2002, operators again began to shut-in production. Latest reports indicate that about 95 percent of crude oil and 75 percent of natural gas production remain shut down. This shutdown will likely continue through Friday,

October 4, 2002, at which time workers will begin returning to facilities for damage assessment and to restore production.

With over 4,000 oil and gas platforms in the Gulf of
Mexico operating on a 24-hour basis, storm events, such as
Isidore and Lili, disrupt a significant sector of the domes-
tic energy supply.

—U.S. Department of the Interior
Minerals Management Service news release

We were early in our long bets on natural gas, but never in history—to that point—had there been back-to-back storms like
those two going right "up the gut" through the "heart of the Gulf's
natural gas production." Instantaneous communication was key to
how we analyzed the situation. The world has come a long way
from the days when I had to run a cable from a brokerage firm to
my office upstairs to get stock quotes, or when in the 1980s, the
seven helicopters Mesa had under contract would be dispatched to
take film photographs of hurricane damage in the Gulf. Today information is instantaneous and extensive. We could immediately see
the havoc of the hurricanes: the twisted and mangled rigs and tem-
porarily evacuated platforms. When those storms hit, much of the
production was shut down. That production would not be made
up, and our fund benefited from the resulting higher prices. The
price of natural gas began to rise just off the news of tightened production. We survived the shoulder season, and we were still long
heading into winter.

It wasn't simple luck. It was experience and information. We're
good at weighing all the risks and drivers and handicapping the situation. Major storms are fairly common. But we never would have

counted on back-to-back strikes like that when all our chips were on the table.

Autumn turned to winter, and we stayed firm. We didn't get spooked by temporary ups and downs. We held our long positions. We constantly analyzed supply and demand, weather, and other information during our thrice-daily meetings. At the dinner meetings, our team was growing closer. Because of the storms and the resulting interruption of natural gas supplies, this was shaping up to be an exciting winter for BP Capital.

We don't consider ourselves traders; we're in most of our positions for the long run. We're always looking twelve months or more out. Less gas in storage because of the hurricanes, coupled with a cold winter, would drive the price up—way up. It was November 2002, and our thinking was a year ahead. "Even if we don't get a supercold winter, we think there will be problems filling natural gas storage for the winter of 2003."

The twin hurricanes had brought us some profits, but our energy fund was still down $31 million going into December. Our Christmas party was a little flat. But I was not ready to play the Grinch. I knew the fundamentals were in our favor. The storms had disrupted production, and gas in storage was being drawn down because of an early start to the winter, causing gas prices to rise. I had to rally our team. At our Christmas party, I was so sure of our decision that I said I was preparing a "good news letter" to our investors.

"I'm going to predict that we will be profitable at the end of the year," I said.

I had shown the letter to Bobby Stillwell before it went out. "You're really sticking your neck out."

"Hell," I said, "my neck's already out there."

It was no small bet. To pull it off, we would have to earn back more than $30 million. This probably wasn't the best prediction to make with so little time left in the year. It was like Babe Ruth pointing to the center field wall and calling a home run with the wind blowing in his face. I felt confident in our analysis, just as Babe had had confidence in his hitting ability.

We were so convinced that we didn't take profits, and we actually increased our position. Winter hit like a sledgehammer. We were in the right position at the right time. The colder it got, the hotter we were. Entering December, the fund was down $31 million. The fund earned $87 million in December. We finished the year up $56 million, a vindication of the letter I had written our investors after the Christmas party. Only one investor responded to my called shot. I'm sure it would have been a very different story if I had struck out.

By January 2003, the thermometer was dropping and gas prices were rising. By then, we'd upped the ante even more. Ron Bassett and I were giving Michael Ross buy orders almost every day. Soon we had 30,000 natural gas contracts. Let me give you an idea of how much money we were dealing with. At that time, 30,000 gas contracts represented $1.5 billion worth of gas. For every $1 move in the price of gas, the fund would make or lose $300 million. We were playing for high stakes.

Michael Ross and I were in New York when it began snowing horizontally. Gas was $5. By the end of January, we were up $89 million for the year. And there was a lot of winter left. The technical traders, who rely on their computers to tell them when to buy or sell, were taking profits. Even though the price was going up rapidly, we could see that the fundamentals were setting up for an even bigger move. So we kept buying while most people were backing away. Most traders felt it was too late to make a play—sort of like investors who back off after a stock has had a big run. Based on all of our calculations and information, we felt the gas market was going to get even hotter.

The temperatures continued to drop into late January 2003. A massive cold-weather pattern was locked in place, which transported Arctic air across most of the United States. The longer the pattern was in place, the more gas the country was pulling from storage. As each week passed, the amount of gas being burned got higher and higher, and prices kept going up.

The bone-snapping cold, labor strikes in Venezuela, and escalating tension in the Middle East were pushing prices to near record levels. There was a growing fear that the United States would attack Iraq. But, as always, the biggest factor was weather. Arctic temperatures were putting the big freeze over much of the country. It wasn't just the cold temperatures. Record snowfalls were making life miserable, particularly for those in the northeast, where, based on the average December through February temperature, they were having one of the coldest (and snowiest) winters on record. Even the Southern states were getting hit. "The eastern two-thirds of the nation was gripped by a bitterly cold air mass that endangered Florida's citrus crop, choked northern harbors with ice, and left residents of North Carolina's Outer Banks digging out of up to a foot of snow," Associated Press and other weather groups reported.

Those who fled to their winter hideaways in places like South Florida didn't get much relief. "In West Palm Beach, Fla., the 35-degree reading was a record, and a combination of cold and wind made it feel like it was in the teens across central Florida," read one report. People were trading shorts for overcoats in Orlando. The

Plains states were downright miserable. "The cold was suspected of causing a major highway bridge in Kansas City, Mo., to buckle, closing a route used by 94,000 cars every day," the *New York Times* reported. "In Minnesota, the coldest winter in two years continued with highs of 10 below zero." And the weather forecasters were predicting that the big chill would continue. Doesn't sound like global warming here.

It was the beginning of the greatest bull market in natural gas. But I'll never forget a phone call that came from a bar on a Saturday night. As I've said, we get information wherever we can. This came from two analysts we use, who had apparently enjoyed a few too many. "We're gonna run out of gas!" one of them screamed to Michael Ross. "We don't have enough gas to get through the winter! Where's Boone? *Where's Boone?* We gotta tell him... *We are going to run out of gas!*"

"Boone's at the ranch with Warren Mitchell," Michael said, referring to the chairman of our Clean Energy natural gas fueling company and the former head of Southern California Gas Company.

"Can we bother him?" the analyst asked.

"*Hell, yes!* He wants to know everything," Michael said.

They called, and I listened. After I heard their story, I called Michael and told him to start buying as soon as the market opened on Sunday night. The home heating market was a potential train wreck based on the wintry weather. Our supply-and-demand forecast models were showing that if winter did not relent, the country could actually do exactly what the guys on the phone had predicted: run out of natural gas. We were facing an all-out shortage. For us, that meant there was no limit to where the price might go.

At this point, we had already made a lot of money. The March gas price was at an all-time high. Most traders would have been happy taking a profit and running. When the majority saw that natural gas was up 25 cents, they cashed in.

I don't believe in taking a little profit when the fundamentals indicate that there's a lot more left on the table. Our analysis indicated that the play was just beginning. Even when the price got to $6 in February 2003—double what it had been in August 2002—we kept buying. Then, as Michael Ross likes to say, "BOOM! The Polar Pig came down."

It was a massive cold-air mother lode of a weather system, and our six weather forecasters were tracking its every move. Since natural gas prices are so hitched to weather, these forecasts are a key part of our analysis. When the price of natural gas hit $7, we were still buying. Then, on February 24, 2003, Dallas literally froze over. We spent four days coated in a thick glaze of ice. The American natural gas commodity market froze up with it.

It was "limit up," the maximum price allowed on a futures contract. The exchange set daily price limits for each individual commodity. Back then, the daily limit for natural gas was a $3 move, up or down. On February 24, 2003, the natural gas market settled at $9.137. The next morning the overnight electronic market was trading limit up, north of $12. To prevent panic, trading was temporarily halted until the price settled down. It rarely happens, but it did in February 2003. The sharp rise in natural gas prices across the United States during the week of February 24 also sparked a federal investigation into commodity futures trading, but they found no evidence of market manipulation. It was just colder than a witch's tit.

It's said that trading commodities is a zero-sum game. For every buyer there's a seller. Some people were caught short, while others simply didn't have the physical gas to deliver to their customers. That's one reason the price spiked as it did; those who sold gas futures, in hopes of buying them back at a lower price, were squeezed. Many of them only had one way out of their losing positions: to buy. Even though the price was up $3, they were spooked that it might climb even higher, which it easily could have done. Since the spike occurred in the last three days of the contract, speculators who were short the spreads or just short the market might have needed to cover their positions because the contract was rolling off. They were covering a short, and as the market continued to go higher, they were being punished on their remaining open positions. As the price continued to escalate, they lost more money. The market continued to go straight up, rewarding the longs.

The price got as high as $13. We let our contracts just roll off or expire as usual at month's end, taking our profits. By the end of February, our fund was up another $300 million, a 330 percent return in two months.

The natural gas market is not a game of chance. It is a predictable science, guided by solid fundamentals of supply and demand. It requires hard work, constant analysis, and the willingness to pull the trigger and not be swayed by temporary fluctuations. And it doesn't hurt to get a weather break.

It's interesting that the thing that sank us at Mesa—natural gas—was what made us at BP Capital. Timing is everything. The media noticed.

"The Resurrection of T. Boone Pickens" read the title of one magazine story. "Two years ago, the legendary oilman was divorced, depressed, and discredited," read the subtitle.

"Age Will Be Served" was another title. "T. Boone Pickens is 76 years old. By almost any reckoning, he is the hottest money manager in the world."

"Comeback Kid" read another. "To anyone familiar with the boom and bust history of T. Boone Pickens, the recent successes of the legendary former oilman . . . will come as only mild surprise."

I certainly did not do it alone.

CHAPTER 6

It's All About the Team

Booneism #16: You win with a team, and I'm a good team builder.

"They made lots of jokes as often as not about their ages. They wandered in and out searching for snacks. They kept a constant eye on the big computer screen that tracks the prices of energy stocks and futures contracts. As I watched them, the image that came to mind was that movie from a few years ago, *Space Cowboys,* in which four old codgers, astronauts from an earlier era, have to go up into space one last time to save the world. Boone and his gang are the Wall Street version of *Space Cowboys.* They've all been around the block a few times, but they can still show the young whippersnappers on Wall Street a thing or two. Having the market turn against you—hell, that's just part of the deal sometimes."

— "Return of the Raider: At 73, Former Takeover Artist
T. Boone Pickens Is Doing Deals, Making Big Money,
and Learning—at Long Last—How to Be Happy,"
Fortune *magazine, 2002*

IN A RECENT interview, I told Katherine Burton, a writer for Bloomberg News, about how we work at BP Capital. Someone had asked me, "When you decide to do something, how do you execute a trade?"

"Hell, I tell them to buy a thousand or sell a thousand," I answered.

"Well, who do you call?"

"I don't call anybody. I just walk down the hall and tell them."

"Well, don't you tell them who to call and who to do business with?"

"No, I don't do that."

I'm not sitting there on the trading desk watching the minute aspects of every trade, although I do watch the monitor screens with our positions closely. And I definitely keep up with the action. To execute the actual trade, I rely on my guys, the best I've ever had.

At Mesa, we once had 920 employees. At BP Capital, we began with six people and four rooms. However, the management philosophies that we employed at Mesa still applied at BP Capital, especially this one:

BUILD TEAM SPIRIT BY COACHING YOUR PLAYERS TO WORK TOGETHER

Every year, we take the approach of a football team with a twelve-game season. Each game represents a month of trading. In 2007, our equity fund was down in January, came back in February, and was up every month through December. So we finished the year 11-1. That's the way we talk about it. Every month is like a game, but not like a regular season game. Every month is like the Super Bowl, and everything is about the team. Everyone is a player, and no one is a superstar.

I see my job as that of a coach. I always have. In fact, I almost went to work as a high school basketball coach when I got out of OSU in 1951. Back then, it was really hard to get a job as a geologist, while it was pretty easy to get a job as a high school coach. The year before graduation, I went to see the basketball coach, Mr. Iba. "Pickens, you can come over here, help out in the training room and throw the balls on the court," he said. "If you keep your ears open, you'll learn something about basketball, and I'll get you a job as a basketball coach." I had been around the court before.

Soon after that a high school coaching job came open in Floydada, Texas (Pumpkin Capital of the U.S.A.), for $300 a month. Since school lasted only nine months a year, I planned to run the local swimming pool in the summer. "Keep looking for a job as a geologist," Mr. Iba advised me. About a month or so later, I got a job as a geologist with Phillips Petroleum and went to tell Mr. Iba that I didn't need the coaching job. "OK, you gotta send me a player," he said, meaning that once I was settled somewhere I'd send him a prospect in return for what he had done for me. We shook hands on it. I did find Mr. Iba that player, and his name was Mel Wright. I helped influence Mel to go to OSU, where he later sank two free throws to beat Kansas University when they had the great Wilt Chamberlain.

DON'T MANAGE, LEAD

Leadership is the quality that transforms good intentions into positive action. It turns a group of individuals into a cohesive unit. You don't manage people, you manage things. I never consciously try to manage anyone. Communication is the key. Leading people is like raising money. It's easier to get people to give money to your cause if you dig deep into your own pocket first. In the same way, people tend to follow your lead if you set a good example.

When my guys see me working hard, they do the same. You won't make it in our organization if you aren't a worker. Years ago I was interviewing a candidate for a VP job who said, "The position doesn't have a good job description. I'm not sure I'll be challenged." I assured him that would not be a problem. The people who work for me don't have to worry about challenges. Hard work is demanded, but the rewards are proportionate. I hire the best people, regardless of age. I pay them well. I give them the best equipment, and I provide the best working environment. I stand behind them, and it shows. Loyalty is a two-way street, and we've been rewarded with an employee turnover rate of almost zero. We don't ever lose anybody we want to keep.

CONCENTRATE ON ACHIEVING GOALS, NOT INCREASING THE SIZE OF THE ORGANIZATION

Our youngest member is David Meaney. He's thirty-two. David began trading stocks and bonds during his senior year in college. After getting a degree in finance from Louisiana Tech University, he worked for seven years as a sales and portfolio trader. He was determined to work for an energy-related hedge fund. After hearing about the success we were having at BP Capital, he sent us his résumé.

David told Michael Ross that he wanted to join our *team* of traders.

Michael said, "Well, there's only one trader—me."

"You guys are managing four and a half billion dollars, and you have only one trader?"

"Right," Michael told him.

David was convinced that he was the right person to become

The Kelker Street boys. We thought we were the toughest bunch in town. That's me on the big bicycle with my cousin Billy Bob Reed sitting behind me. *(T. Boone Pickens Archives)*

Baby Boone with his beautiful mother, Grace Molonson Pickens. *(T. Boone Pickens Archives)*

My dad was a member of Sigma Alpha Epsilon at Cumberland University in Tennessee. He came to Stillwater in 1949 on the day I was initiated into the fraternity at Oklahoma A&M (now Oklahoma State). *(T. Boone Pickens Archives)*

One of Tough Gut's teams. Coach T. G. Hull (in suit, far left of back row) led the Amarillo High Golden Sandstorm forever. I'm front and center, number 13. *(T. Boone Pickens Archives)*

My first job in the oil business was pumping gas at Ray Smith's Sinclair station in Holdenville in 1940. Fifty years later I'm still pumping away at Mesa's first natural gas station in Phoenix at Sky Harbor Airport. *(T. Boone Pickens Archives)*

I invited the press to my home in Dallas to see how easy it is to refuel a natural-gas-powered vehicle. It was a convenience ahead of its time. *(T. Boone Pickens Archives)*

Here I am opening the first meeting of the United Shareholders Association. Most CEOs forget that it's the shareholders who own the companies. CEOs are just employees, but they sure don't like to be told so.
(T. Boone Pickens Archives)

U nited
S hareholders
A ssociation

"*T*he United Shareholders Association will focus attention on the lack of management accountability and support constructive changes to restore America's competitiveness."

T. Boone Pickens
USA Kickoff
August 26, 1986

MARCH 4, 1985 $1.95

TIME

U.S. Al
Neighbo
Gridlock

The Takeover Game

Corporate Raider
T. Boone Pickens

This *Time* cover, though flattering, missed the boat. The name of the game wasn't takeovers. It was shareholder value.
(Courtesy of the editors of Time *magazine © 2008 Time Inc.)*

Here I am at the White House in 1987 with America's greatest president and first lady.
(Courtesy of the White House)

Goodbye, Mesa. Hello, BP Capital. My biggest comeback begins at the age of sixty-eight.

Here I am with a few OSU buddies. I've been able to leverage my contributions to my alma mater and generate more than $1 billion for Oklahoma State. *(Phil Shockley/Oklahoma State University)*

Below: I've also given $100 million to the University of Texas system, to be split equally between the M. D. Anderson Cancer Center in Houston and UT Southwestern Medical Center in Dallas (shown here). They have twenty-five years to grow my gift to $1 billion. If they don't, whatever they've earned goes to OSU. That's some incentive. *(T. Boone Pickens Archives)*

I've made large investments in the huge Suncor operation in the oil sands outside Fort McMurray, Alberta, Canada. Here I'm joined by my good friend of fifty years Harley Hotchkiss on a visit to the company.
(T. Boone Pickens Archives)

Karen and Andrew Littlefair join me and my wife, Madeleine, at the listing of Clean Energy on the NASDAQ in 2007. CLNE is the eighth company I've taken public.
(T. Boone Pickens Archives)

Touring the Horse Hollow wind farm outside Sweetwater, Texas. At this time, Horse Hollow is the world's largest wind farm, but our Pampa project will be several times its size.
(T. Boone Pickens Archives)

Now that Madeleine is by my side, my comeback is complete.
(Oklahoma Heritage Foundation)

Madeleine and me visiting the Great Wall of China in 2007, during my first and last trip to that country.
(T. Boone Pickens Archives)

Madeleine and me in front of the Burj Al Arab hotel in 2007, on my first and last trip to Dubai.
(T. Boone Pickens Archives)

The view from my
Mesa Vista Ranch
across the Canadian
River Valley at my
old friend Harold
Courson's ranch.
(Wyman Meinzer)

The quail hunting on the Mesa Vista is world class.
Here I am out in the field looking for a downed bird.
(Wyman Meinzer)

The president and the first lady invited Madeleine and
me to the White House in 2007 for the state dinner
for Queen Elizabeth and Prince Philip.
(Courtesy of the White House)

our second trader, and he kept calling Michael to make sure he got the message. Although he hadn't traded oil or natural gas before, he was smart and eager to learn. We felt that was enough, and David Meaney became our second trader.

You can't measure a business by its size. Big isn't necessarily better in most operations. We always worked shorthanded at Mesa. No bureaucracy. We cut office politics down to zero and gave people the greatest opportunities to advance. Big corporations rarely run efficiently. They can build an assembly line, but they can't modify it when conditions warrant. Their executives are typically isolated and insulated from what's happening a few floors—and in many cases a few buildings—away. You can find plenty of proof in the U.S. auto industry. They've closed auto plants and laid off armies of workers. The industry invented in America was invaded by foreign competitors who were more efficient and quicker to react. It is also true that revolutionary ideas typically come from small new companies such as Apple and Google, where people see their work not as jobs but as missions. We were on a mission when we left Mesa. At our new company, BP Capital, the six of us concentrated on a single goal: to have a 12-0 season in the commodities market.

FIND PEOPLE WHO CAN DO A JOB BETTER THAN YOU CAN—THEN LET THEM DO THAT JOB

As I've said, age is just a number. I love to give people, especially young people, a chance. I'm biased toward youth, but I also think youth is a state of mind. I'm interested in whether a person can do the job. Regardless of age, I'm looking for people with the potential to do a job better than I can. When I find them, I give them the job and then go do something else. There is plenty of work for everybody.

My current team is the best I have assembled in my half century in business. It has twelve members of varied ages, backgrounds, and experience. Again, to use the sports metaphor, it's like building a great football or basketball squad: you need some rookies and some veterans. Teams composed exclusively of all-stars rarely shine. You need a mix of skills, with each member having his or her own strength.

In any business, people are the greatest commodity, and two of our veterans—Bobby Stillwell and Ron Bassett—are two of the best. Bobby has been with me since the early 1960s. By 2001, he was sixty-five and facing mandatory retirement at his Houston law firm, Baker & Botts. Bobby has never been the retiring type. He is like me. We both need the money.

"I have to be out of there by the end of 2001," he told me one day.

"Do you know what you're going to do?"

"No," he said. "I'm going to do something, but I don't know what."

"Well, we've always talked about doing something together. Let's do it now!"

Although Bobby didn't know exactly what he would be doing at BP Capital, there was never any doubt that he would have plenty to do. "Even if you didn't have anything to do in the morning, by 10 a.m. you'd be busy," Bobby likes to say of both the old days and today. He is the chief compliance officer for the equity fund and an adviser on everything. He's our lead duck on our wind and water projects.

Ron has been with me since the cattle days in 1969. He has so much experience in so many areas that he can cover any base, and he plays a vital role. I take Ron's counsel to heart, like the time he suggested we hire an attorney here in Dallas named Sandy Campbell. Ron had worked with Sandy on several occasions, and he liked what he saw. Soon he had Sandy working on deals for us. In 2004, Ron told me that it was time to bring Sandy on board full-time. He's now become one of our key players. These days, if it takes place on my Mesa Vista Ranch, Sandy handles the negotiations as well as the contract. He does the same with my oil and gas operations and my jet. He's the kind of utility player a team like BP Capital relies on.

Dick Grant has been with me for twenty-seven years. He was one of the youngest members when he first came to Mesa in 1981 after graduating from West Texas State University to work in the accounting department. When I started BP Capital, he had a difficult time deciding whether to accept the job I had offered him. "I'm not sure what decision you think you have to make," I told him. "You can either stay in Amarillo or move to Dallas and work with me and get a generous severance from Mesa." He took the job, collected the severance, and moved to Dallas in 1997 to become controller. Today Dick is chief financial officer of BP Capital and responsible for accounting, reporting, and all administrative functions for our funds.

Did you see my interview on CNBC? Or read the article in *The Wall Street Journal,* where I predicted a swing in the price of oil? That's Jay Rosser at work. Jay juggles the hundreds of media requests we receive. He schedules my speaking engagements. And he also handles all of BP Capital's public affairs. Jay came to Mesa after working with Texas governor Bill Clements during his second term in Austin. After I left Mesa in 1996, Jay went to work with Koch Industries in Wichita, Kansas. It wasn't until 2003 that I was able to talk him back to Texas and BP Capital. Jay's office is right next to mine, and he travels with me most of the time.

Bobby, Ron, Sandy, and Dick bring stability to our organization. We're able to manage so many projects and investments with only a core group of people because everyone has worked together for years and, in some cases, decades.

Hunger, drive, and sheer natural talent can be every bit as valuable as age.

Alex Szewczyk was born in Poland. He was working on his MBA at Southern Methodist University when he started cold-calling our office, hoping to get a job. He later told me that he became determined to work for us after studying Mesa's attempt to take over Gulf Oil, which has been part of the curriculum at many business schools.

Alex called my assistant, Sally Geymüller, for three months before he got in to meet with me. When we finally sat down, he'd worked up an intriguing pitch.

"Mr. Pickens, I'm still in business school. I don't have that much experience. But I'm a very hard worker," he said. "In fact, I'll work for free, and if you don't like the results you see from me, you won't owe me anything." I sent Alex to talk to the other guys, and they agreed that he was serious and smart. He looked like he was our kind of guy, so in 2001 Alex became a junior analyst. Now he and Brian Bradshaw run the equity fund.

A few years later, we were interviewing for an accounting position, and we had two candidates. We hired them both: Danny Tillett for the accounting position and Brian Bradshaw as an equity fund analyst. Danny, thirty-five, already had a solid track record with us. After graduating from Stephen F. Austin State University, he had gone to work in the Houston office of Arthur Andersen as a tax accountant, handling my personal taxes. It was a natural fit for him to come and work for BP Capital. His tax strategies have saved us millions of dollars. Brian, thirty-two, has an accounting degree from Texas A&M, and he was surprised at how quickly he would be helping run a multibillion-dollar equity fund. Brian wasn't a rookie when he showed up. He had been through a tough period in his career and had also worked for Arthur Andersen during the whole Enron mess, which drove the huge accounting firm out of business.

In 2004, I put Alex and Brian in charge of our equity fund. Although people were surprised that I put them into the position as soon as I did, I never had any doubts about what they could do. Obviously I liked these guys, and I wanted to give them an opportunity. Alex later joked that he wondered if I was really just giving them enough rope to hang themselves. I like people who haven't developed a lot of bad habits. They tend to listen better and think more clearly.

HELP, DON'T HINDER. LET YOUR PEOPLE SUCCEED.

You don't set up people to fail. Sure, you challenge them. You make them earn their stripes. I think there is enough success and enough money for all of us. It wasn't a huge risk for us to give Brian and Alex a shot at running our equity fund. We are there every step of the way. They do the analysis, make recommendations, and manage the fund.

Managing the equity fund is an open process. Everyone brings ideas to the table. Everyone's ideas are considered, and everyone participates in the decision-making process. You can't criticize anyone for making a bad decision, because we're all involved.

Alex and Brian invest in energy-sector stocks—everything from oil companies to alternative energy to petrochemicals to coal. Ninety percent of the fund is invested in energy equities; the other 10 percent is invested in energy futures, whose positions are similar to those of our energy fund. Like our energy fund, the equity investments are guided by our constant analysis of the fundamentals. Proof of my well-placed faith came at the end of 2004, Alex and Brian's first year at the helm. The BP Capital Energy Equity Fund was up 115 percent. Not bad for their first year.

FREQUENTLY, THE BEST PERSON FOR THE JOB IS RIGHT UNDER YOUR NOSE

Sally Geymüller is another one of our key members, just waiting for the opportunity to perform. Sally, who runs the office at BP Capital, has been with me for thirty years—and she's still in her forties. A *Dallas Morning News* reporter was surprised that our group seemed to be all men. I quickly pointed out, "Sally Geymüller runs the organization."

She was a senior in high school in Canyon, Texas, when her father died unexpectedly. Her mother, who had never worked outside the home, had to find a job to support her three teenagers. Sally herself had to find a job immediately after graduation. Her mother had a close friend who was the secretary of a Mesa vice president. She got Sally an interview, and Sally got a job.

She was seventeen and began working part-time in Mesa's central records department. Determined to get a college education, she applied for a government grant to attend West Texas State University. She joined us full-time after graduating. She then worked her way up and eventually became the assistant to my secretary. This was in the 1980s, and we had a lot going on. I asked Trixie Lee Slife, one of Mesa's first employees, to come out of retirement and run the office while we searched for a new secretary.

Instead, Trixie saw that Sally had talent. She became her mentor. We hired a new secretary. Our new secretary didn't last long, and

Trixie told me that Sally was ready for the job. She moved with me to Dallas in 1989.

> **Booneism #17:** *Play by the rules. It's no fun to win if you cheat.*

WHETHER IT'S THE oil business or commodities, there are always opportunities to cheat. I would rather play by the rules and lose than win by cheating. There are three things that will end a career with me. I will not tolerate drinking on the job, stealing, or carrying on an interoffice relationship. Any one of those three is disruptive and damaging to the operation. These three rules are well known and understood throughout the organization. If you hope to be in a business long term, you don't take shortcuts. If you aren't happy in what you do, find something else.

GIVE AS MANY EMPLOYEES A STAKE IN THE BUSINESS AS POSSIBLE

Those who have a strong financial stake in a business tend to think and act like owners. At Mesa, 95 percent of our employees owned stock in the company. *Money* magazine listed our benefits package among the ten best plans in the country—better than any other oil company. *Forbes* listed Mesa at the top in net income per employee for two straight years. I'm proud of that record and can only wish that it existed everywhere.

ENCOURAGE CONSTANT, UNINHIBITED, AND OPEN TWO-WAY COMMUNICATION

Ours is a confident and cohesive group. People are not shy about expressing opinions. We all get into the office early. We usually eat breakfast together. We always have lunch together, too. At least once a month, we have dinner together. We have our daily Investment Committee meetings in our conference room, sometimes two or three times a day. We meet again after the close of the markets each day from 4 p.m. until around 6 p.m. This sounds like an awful lot of meetings, but we really do work well together, exchange a lot of information, and enjoy being with one another. All of this reinforces our strength. Although our goal is to reach an agreement among the group, I'm the decision maker, if I have to be. More often than not, I don't have to be.

I'm a believer in informal communication within the company. Our public affairs director, Jay Rosser, says I would have been a good reporter or editor, because I work the beat constantly. I don't do e-mail and don't understand the appeal of text messaging. I like to pick up the phone or walk into someone's office. Writing is great for records and details. People respond best to conversation. Talking generates ideas and makes companies—and individuals—grow. Back in 1956, when I started my first company, Petroleum Exploration, Inc., I posted each day's correspondence on a clipboard in the office. That way everyone could see the inner workings of the company. At BP Capital, things are equally transparent. You don't have to rise through endless levels of bureaucracy to be informed or to get to me. When you show me that you can do a job, I will give you the opportunity to do it by providing you with all the information we have, and I will also make myself available.

It has to be a two-way flow of information. I want to know what my people are hearing, reading, and thinking. If they aren't talking to me, I'll ask them. And they know that I listen to them. When I'm traveling, I'll take the time to talk for an hour or so about what is going on. My most famous line in the office is "Have you got anything?" I'm always available, in the office or by phone, and that makes it easy for everyone to talk to me. Not every conversation leads to a decision.

LEAD BUT ALSO LISTEN

A real leader never leads by fear. I develop a rapport so no one is afraid to question my opinions or decisions. They do it openly but respectfully, and I welcome it. The best way to avoid confusion, misconceptions, and disasters is to have that fearless, open discussion. If someone is afraid of me or afraid of making a mistake, they might be unwilling to speak up and provide critical information. You can't afford that, especially in a high-stakes business like ours.

I can veto ideas, but that rarely happens. What we sometimes disagree on is timing. It's not if, but when. I usually want to do something faster than others may want to do it. Still, we listen to each other. I hear people out, and they hear me out. It's no secret that some of the biggest mistakes I've made were the result of my impatience. So I am more than willing to listen.

A LEADER KEEPS PEOPLE FOCUSED ON THE FUTURE

After one particularly painful day, I walked into the conference room. "Your faces are so long it would take two barbers to shave each one of you," I told my guys. I thought it was funny, but there wasn't a smile in the room. I then asked them if they were still satisfied with our analysis of the fundamentals. They said they were satisfied we had it right. "Well, if the fundamentals haven't changed, then I'm not going to panic. We'll get it all back soon enough."

A LEADER ENCOURAGES TEAMWORK

My basketball analogies are not merely figurative. There's a basket-ball court at a school next door to our office. Three or four days a week, after the markets close, my guys suit up and head out to play. On the court, they exhibit what makes them work so well at the office: a diverse collection of talents, seamlessly working together, each player accentuating the others, no man for himself alone but for the team as a whole. Our young guys do an excellent job of ana-lyzing the market and assembling the information from various con-sultants. I trust our people, but the record we have makes it easy to trust them.

CHAPTER 7

Learning to Live with Peak Oil

Booneism #18: I may have been born at night, but it wasn't last night.

AFTER A HALF century in the oil and gas business, I've learned a lot of lessons. Few have been cheap. I understand how difficult it is to find oil. I know how fast it begins to decline once you find it. But many of the lessons I learned aren't about wells or fields or deals. They are about the forces that move markets and drive economic change.

Leading this list is one all-important truth: the world is running out of cheap oil. It's a finite and diminishing resource. Despite the best efforts of wildcatters, producers, major oil companies, and OPEC, we are finding far less and needing much more. The numbers are staggering. Total global production is presently at about 85 million barrels a day, a combination of 72 million barrels of black oil, 11 million barrels of natural gas liquids, another 2 million in refinery process gains, and stock liquids. Next quarter, demand is expected to grow to 87 million barrels a day. It's going to be hard to cover 87 with 85. Since we will be using 2 million barrels more each day than we produce, inventories are being drawn down. If you produce 85 million barrels a day and multiply that by 365 days, you get 30 billion barrels of oil produced globally each year. Yet new discoveries can't keep pace with the growing global demand. Projections are that by 2025, we'll be using 120 million barrels a day—more than twice what we have the capacity to produce. All I can say is that it will be impossible to produce that much oil.

Global demand is soaring, yet global production is flat, and difficult, at best, to keep at present levels. The key to understanding this predicament is called Peak Oil. It's a theory that's been around for a long time, and now it's a reality we are all forced to face.

The Peak Oil theory was established by Texas-born Shell geophysicist Marion King Hubbert, who created a model of, and a theory about, the world's dwindling oil reserves. In 1956, he told members of the American Association of Petroleum Geologists (AAPG) something nobody wanted to hear, either today or back then: oil production from conventional sources would peak in the United States by the early 1970s. He also predicted that global oil production would peak in about fifty years, or roughly around 2006. According to Hubbert's Peak Oil theory, at that time the world's oil production would then go into a state of permanent decline.

Hubbert hit it right on the nose. U.S. oil production did in fact peak in 1970. Domestic production was at an all-time high— 10 million barrels a day. Today we produce half that amount.

What happens when the Peak Oil scenario finally becomes reality on a global scale? It should come as no surprise that doomsday scenarios are commonplace. Here's one:

Starting in 2010, no later than 2020 or 2030, according to the latest vision of secular apocalypse, global oil supplies will peak, and the world will begin to unravel at the seams. . . . And when the truth can no longer be obscured, the price will spike, the economy nosedive, and the underpinnings of our civilization will start tumbling like dominos. The U.S.—Consumer No. 1, in the lingo of [Jeremy] Leggett's book [*The Empty Tank: Oil, Gas, Hot Air, and the Coming Financial Catastrophe*]—will be the most vulnerable, having allowed its citizens to pile up mountains of debt. "The price of houses will collapse. Stock markets will crash. Within a short period, human wealth—little more than a pile of paper at the best of times, even with the confidence about the future high among traders—will shrivel." There will be emergency summits, diplomatic initiatives, urgent exploration efforts, but the turmoil will not subside. Thousands of companies will go bankrupt, and millions will be unemployed. . . .

> —*Jonathon Gatehouse, "When the Oil Runs Out,"* Maclean's

How about another one:

The prospect seems unthinkable—mostly because the consequences, if true, would be unimaginable. Permanent fuel shortages would tip the world into a generations-long economic depression. Millions would lose their jobs as industry implodes. Farm tractors would be idled for lack of fuel, triggering massive famines. Energy wars would flare. . . . This may sound like the plot from a B-grade disaster flick. But with crude prices hitting record highs since 2004, global oil demand outstripping supplies like never before and major discoveries stagnant for 20 years, peak oil has migrated from the fringe to the center of the global energy debate.

—*Pulitzer Prize-winning journalist Paul Salopek, "A Tank of Gas, a World of Trouble,"* Chicago Tribune

What can be done about Peak Oil? It is incumbent upon us to accept and prepare for this reality. The first step is to look behind the smoke and mirrors and learn the truth about what is really happening in our Peak Oil world. The second step is better management of resources, new and creative forms of energy exploration, and bringing alternatives on line as fast as possible.

WE HAVE TO STOP SLEEPWALKING

In late 2007 the former chairman of Shell, Lord Oxburgh, predicted that the price of oil could hit $150 per barrel as the oil industry kept its "head in the sand" about the depletion of supplies. "We may be sleepwalking into a problem that is actually going to be very serious, and it may be too late to do anything about it by the time we are fully aware," he said.

You can bet your ass we are going to be too late.

Friends and critics alike in Washington and throughout the country have been telling me I should "just quit talking about higher energy prices." They say that people like me are "the ones moving oil prices up." Nobody can do that. What we need is more straight talk and less baloney. Our failure to talk frankly about, much less address head-on, this obvious supply-and-demand problem only postpones the inevitable.

President George W. Bush signed an energy bill in December 2007, which mandated that 35 billion gallons of renewable fuel be blended into the fuel supply by 2022 to reduce our dependency on imported oil. Of that amount, 21 billion gallons would have to come from sources other than corn, such as wood chips. A more likely source would be natural gas, not wood chips. Can we do it in that time frame? I don't think so. We can't loosen this noose. We are going to be dependent on oil for at least another fifty years; that means foreign oil, and that means trouble. Either we need to be prepared to face those consequences or we need to get working on some alternatives.

ALL THE LOW-HANGING FRUIT HAS BEEN PICKED

Whether you are an independent oilman or a major oil company, you go after the biggest and best reserves as quickly as you can. Nobody in the oil business believes in saving the best for last.

I asked a Shell geologist friend recently, "Jerry, you've been around the world looking for oil your entire career. Have you ever looked for oil someplace where nobody had been before?"

Jerry is in his sixties, and he thought about it for two seconds. "No, Boone, I've never been anyplace where there hadn't already been geologists before me." I'm older than Jerry, and I've also never been anyplace where someone hasn't already been before in the pursuit of oil. Every conceivable place has been looked at. The world has been turned upside down in the search for oil. Having said this, there is still going to be oil found around the world. But it will be much more expensive to find and produce.

AMERICA DOESN'T CONTROL THE OIL INDUSTRY—
OR THE PRICE OF OIL

Seventy-five percent of the world's oil is in the hands of state-owned oil companies. They have one motive: to get the best price for their oil. Not unfair. Not unreasonable. Just a fact.

When we look at the list of countries from which we import oil—Canada, Mexico, Saudi Arabia, Nigeria, Kuwait, Venezuela, and Russia—we have only one friend: Canada. Mexico and Kuwait are neutral at best.

The United States is currently using 21 million barrels of oil a day and producing only 5.5 million. We consume almost 25 percent of all the oil used in the world daily, even though we represent less than 5 percent of the world's population. America is the world's third-largest producer of oil. Keep in mind, however, that our production is marginal: high cost and low volume. The average oil well in the United States produces less than five barrels a day. Compare that with the average oil well in Saudi Arabia: 3,000 barrels a day.

Politicians are notorious for blaming Exxon and the other major oil companies for setting high prices. It's easy to do, given their high profile and hefty profits. Anyone who knows me and knows my history recognizes that I've never been a big fan of Big Oil, but to blame Exxon and the other majors for today's record prices is erroneous and just downright stupid. Exxon produces about 2 percent of global production. *How can a company with just 2 percent of the world's production be setting the price of anything?* It's a ridiculous argument, but Congress is intent on blaming somebody for something that it should have addressed years ago.

I see the major oil companies as very important to the United States and its energy security. Most of their money is made in overseas operations. They pay huge taxes domestically. And they provide thousands of jobs here at home. Who owns them? Not their management. Management owns very little. It's your neighbors next door. Big Oil is owned by millions of individual stockholders, key pension funds, and almost everyone's 401(k). Technically they are far superior to state-owned oil companies with one all-important exception: they don't have the oil.

I suggest that instead of singling out Big Oil as our problem, we take a closer look at the world's two largest oil producers: Saudi Arabia and Russia. The Saudis and the Russians recently announced that they are starting to talk in their shared quest to "stabilize" oil prices. *Do you believe that?* I don't. They're not trying to stabilize a thing. They're trying to get the best price for their oil. Why wouldn't they want high oil prices? Who wants to sell their resources on the cheap? They've got a finite, dwindling natural resource. Once they produce it, it's gone forever.

King Abdullah of Saudi Arabia has already put us on notice. In April 2008, he confirmed that new oil discoveries in his family's kingdom would remain untapped in order to preserve oil wealth for future generations of Saudis.

"I have no secret from you that when there were some new finds, I told them, 'No. Leave it in the ground. With grace of God, our children need it,' " he said in remarks on April 12. This was all predictable.

President Bush has already learned this lesson. During his Middle East trip in May 2008, he asked King Abdullah to increase oil production as a way for the United States to combat soaring energy costs. The king turned him down, a fact that led *The Wall Street Journal* to pen a scathing editorial titled "Beseeching the Saudis":

The same request by Mr. Bush had already been rebuffed by the Saudis during his visit to Riyadh in January. This time around, the Saudi response was particularly blunt and condescending: "If you want more oil, you need to buy it," said Ali al-Naimi, the Saudi oil minister.

When you consider the fact that the Russians are also making deals with the Iranians, and that the two countries are the world's number one and number two in natural gas reserves, that's even more alarming. So now the Russians are tied up with both the Saudis for oil production and the Iranians for gas production. Where does the United States fit in in all of this?

You'll pardon the expression, but my answer is, Sucking hind tit.

TOO LITTLE, TOO LATE

The first commercial oil well dates back to 1859. The last major find was in 2000—the Kashagan field in the Caspian Sea, which was considered to be the fifth-largest oil field in the world. The field is said to be capable of producing over 1 million barrels of crude daily when it goes into production in the next decade. Of similar size, Prudhoe Bay, discovered in 1976 in Alaska, produced 2 million barrels a day at its peak. One of the problems with major discoveries is the amount of time it takes them to become producing oil fields. Even if we find a field, such as the Tupi field discovered in 2007 by Petrobras in Brazil, it can take ten years before there is production online.

I'm convinced that some of the oil that people claim is still out there might not be all that it is cracked up to be. Twenty years ago, on a trip to Alaska, I visited with that state's former governor Wally Hickel, who also is a former U.S. Secretary of the Interior. Hickel claimed back then that untapped oil reserves in the Arctic National Wildlife Refuge (ANWR) were more than 2 billion barrels. More

recently I've heard other politicians say that there are 16 billion barrels in that protected reserve. Somehow Hickel's 2 billion barrels
mushroomed. I thought Hickel's estimate was in the ballpark. Even
if there is anything close to 16 billion barrels out there, the Alaska
pipeline can haul only 2 million barrels a day. And forget about
building a new pipeline; that will never happen. There's no reason
to build a new pipeline anyway. You can get the oil out over time
and preserve the field longer, if it is larger than I think it will be.

The Alaska pipeline, which once operated at capacity at 2 million barrels a day, carries less than half of that today. Some people
like to say our problem is a lack of refining capacity. It's a myth.
Who needs new refineries if you don't have oil to refine? There
hasn't been a new refinery built in the United States since 1976.
New refineries will come online, but they'll be overseas. In 2006,
Wood Mackenzie Consultants Ltd. estimated there are five hundred
expansion projects, including sixty-six new refineries planned in
countries like the United Arab Emirates, Kuwait, and India. There's
no need to add to the refining capacities in the United States. We
don't have the oil, which means that overseas interests will now be
capturing the value of both the oil they produce and the products
they refine. It will be a double dip, and the cost goes up for us.

Meanwhile, some of the world's biggest oil fields are in decline,
including Ghawar in Saudi Arabia, the biggest of all. Add to this
decline the fact that the infrastructure is also aging. It's like a treadmill. Demand keeps ratcheting up, while we're struggling to increase supply. In 2006, British Petroleum had a problem with its
gathering system at Prudhoe Bay and had to shut down the field for
almost a month. And that field is only thirty years old. From an infrastructure standpoint, fields that are older than Prudhoe Bay are in
even worse shape. Get ready for more and more infrastructure

problems, as well as declining production from the fields themselves. Let's face it: everything is getting old.

RESERVE FACTS ARE FICTION

The Saudis claim they have 260 billion barrels in reserve. I don't believe them. I don't think there's any way they have that much oil. The Saudis will also tell you that they'll have 12 million barrels of daily production capacity by 2010 and 15 million by 2015. That's not going to happen either. There's no way to tell what they actually have. They won't let anybody look at the data. Back in the 1970s, our company was the first to have our reserves audited, and we called for the industry to do the same. The biggest asset any oil company has is its reserves. You're going to have your financials audited; why wouldn't you have your reserves? But have any of the state-owned oil companies adopted this practice? Absolutely not. It's interesting how people accept their word. *The Saudis say they've got 260 billion barrels.* I don't believe them.

Reserve estimates for Kuwait, Iran, Iraq, and Saudi Arabia show an alarming trend. Between 1983 and 1987, each of these four country's reserve estimates rose by astonishing percentages; a few years later, some rose even more. In 1983, Kuwait upped their estimates from 65 billion to 99 billion barrels. There's credible evidence that disproves these numbers, such as this 2005 Bloomberg report:

KUWAIT OIL FIELD, WORLD'S SECOND LARGEST, IS "EXHAUSTED"

Kuwaiti oil output from the world's second-largest field
is "exhausted" and falling after almost six decades of

pumping, forcing the government to increase spending on new deposits, the chairman of the state oil company said.

The plateau in output from the Burgan field will be about 1.7 million barrels a day, rather than as much as the 2 million a day that engineers had forecast could be maintained for the rest of the field's 30 to 40 years of life, said Farouk al Zanki, the chairman of the state-owned Kuwait Oil Co.

Two months later, *Petroleum Intelligence Weekly* reported seeing internal Kuwaiti documents that supported only half of the reserves that the country was claiming:

KUWAITI OIL RESERVES MAY BE
HALF OFFICIAL ESTIMATE, WEEKLY SAYS

Kuwait's oil reserves may be half the official estimate of 99 billion barrels, *Petroleum Intelligence Weekly* reported, citing data it had seen from Kuwait Oil Company, the state oil company.

Kuwait's remaining proven- and non-proven oil reserves are about 48 billion barrels, *Petroleum Intelligence* said. The Burgan Oilfield, the world's second biggest after Saudi Arabia's Ghawar, holds 20 billion barrels, and 17 billion barrels are in the country's north, the report said. The fields contain proven and non-proven reserves . . .

—*Bloomberg News, January 23, 2006*

In 1986, Iran upped its estimates from about 60 billion barrels to about 90 billion barrels. Then in 2001 those same reserves grew again, from 90 billion to almost 140 billion. Not to be outdone, Iraq increased its reserve estimates in 1986 from 50 billion barrels to 100 billion. The Saudis upped their reserve estimates in 1987 from 170 billion to 260 billion barrels.

There was no basis in fact for these increases. All this happened without any drilling. No question these are the cheapest barrels of oil ever found. Ghawar, the giant oil field in Saudi Arabia that ranks as the largest field in the world, has now produced 60 billion barrels. Discovered in 1948, it accounts for more than half of Saudi Arabia's cumulative oil production. At its peak in 1981, Ghawar produced 5.7 million barrels a day, the highest sustained oil production rate ever achieved by a single oil field. Raising their reserves from 170 to 260 billion barrels is like the Saudis saying they have discovered one and a half additional Ghawars. That's highly unlikely. Many of us in the industry refer to these unusual increases in reserves as "paper barrels." Over time, the paper barrels have been accepted as fact. I think they're fiction. These increases happened at a time when there was no exploration activity. And let's not forget, none of these reserves has been subject to outside audit. If I'm right, this issue is a lot more serious than you can imagine.

The truth? Their fields are in decline. The Saudis are now lifting about six barrels of water for every one barrel of oil they pump out of the ground. To keep reservoir pressure high, they are injecting as much as 15 to 18 million barrels of water into their wells a day. The Russians are faced with a similar plight. The second-largest oil producer in the world, Russia is now lifting nine barrels of water to each barrel of oil. This leads me to believe they've got serious problems maintaining their production. It's mature and no longer increasing. All these wonderful oil fields have peaked and are already in decline.

**EACH YEAR AMERICANS SPEND MORE THAN HALF
A TRILLION DOLLARS ON FOREIGN OIL: WE'VE
CREATED AN ECONOMIC MONSTER, WHICH WE
ARE NOW LOOKING DIRECTLY IN THE EYE**

During the Arab oil embargo of the 1970s, the United States was importing 25 percent of its oil. During the first Gulf War, that number rose to 42 percent. In 2008, we were importing 65 percent of our oil—75 percent if you include refined products. That number will only grow larger in the future.

This $1-trillion-a-year outflow for the purchase of foreign oil is more than six times the cost of the Iraq war, which runs $150 billion a year. It's the greatest transfer of wealth in human history.

**ARE WE IN JEOPARDY OF FALLING FROM
SUPERPOWER STATUS?**

It's a question I ask myself. We have to act fast, and that means leadership. If we could get the right leadership in Washington, it would make a huge difference. The key is to come up with a plan that stops the transfer of our wealth overseas.

**THE MORE THE OIL-IMPORTING NATIONS COMPETE
WITH ONE ANOTHER, THE HIGHER THE PRICE WILL GO**

One of the big questions today concerns the growing economies—and escalating energy usage—of countries like China and India. Those nations will never utilize fossil fuels to the same degree that we do. Americans on average consume twenty-four barrels of oil per person per year. By comparison, the Chinese consume two barrels per person per year. Clearly there is not enough oil in the world for emerging economies to match America's insatiable demand.

However, China now has an edge on us in the global race for oil, and it's a powerful advantage. The Chinese government owns one-half of the oil they use. They have to import the other half, which makes them the second-largest importer of oil after the United States, and they are very aggressive about securing this other 50 percent. They know that their future depends on procuring this supply. The United States has no similar policy because we don't have state-owned energy companies. Our market-based system faces an uphill battle when competing against countries with state-owned companies. We have to rely on Exxon, Chevron, Valero, and others to procure and process, and to supply domestic markets. These companies are going head-to-head against the Chinese as they secure oil from Canada, Mexico, Saudi Arabia, and other countries. Simultaneously, the major oil companies are also defending themselves before Congress, which continually harasses them. Where does that leave the United States? Once again, sucking hind tit.

How will this play out? It only makes sense that as oil gets even scarcer, and the producing countries step up their requirements for oil, those that have the oil are going to win this battle. This should be yet another wake-up call to pull out all stops in promoting alternative fuels in the United States.

NEW AND IMPROVED TECHNOLOGY CAN'T SAVE THE DAY

In my fifty-six years as a geologist and entrepreneur in the field of energy, I have seen an explosion of new technologies, from satellites to microelectronics. While these technologies have stretched to new levels our reach for sources of oil, we have not needed this technology to find the really big oil fields. Remember, most of them were found twenty-five to fifty years ago.

When I debate Steve Forbes on this subject, he takes the position that new technology will enable us to find oil in places we couldn't go before. Cutting-edge equipment will help you drill fewer dry holes, he argues, and lower the cost of finding oil. I agree, but only to a point. It can help you find new oil but not the big fields. They have already been found. New technologies are simply helping us find smaller targets.

Exxon is better at finding and producing oil than any other company. The company certainly has the technology. But Exxon can't find major new production if it's not there to be found. One CEO once told me there may be as many as 7 trillion barrels left to be discovered and produced. "If it's so easy, why doesn't Exxon increase production?" I asked. "You've been flatlining for ten years. If you've got the oil, show it to us. Tell us, 'Here's a new billion-barrel field.' "

THE PRICE OF OIL CAN ONLY GO UP—
AND THEN UP SOME MORE

The 85 million barrels of oil produced in the world each day is steadily diminishing by a natural decline rate of 5 to 8 percent annually. That means the world loses approximately 5 million barrels a day of production every year. That's a lot, and it's hard to replace. I can't believe we'll ever produce more than 85 million barrels a day. Meanwhile, demand is going to keep moving up. If I'm right on supply and Hubbert's Peak Oil theory is on the money, the only thing that's going to control this market is price. You're thinking, *What's he getting ready to tell me? The price is going up to $200 a barrel?* The answer is, yes, it is. *When?*

Not long ago, I was giving a speech in Charlotte, North Carolina, when a young man raised his hand and asked the question on everyone's mind: "What's going to happen to gasoline prices?"

"First let me ask, how old are you?"

"Twenty-two."

"What's the lowest price you've ever paid for gasoline?"

"A buck twenty-five."

If I had asked that same question of a twenty-two-year-old in Europe, his answer would probably have been around $3 a gallon.

My answer to the question would be the eleven-cent-a-gallon gas I pumped as a kid in Holdenville. When the Texaco station down the street lowered its price from 12 cents to 11.9, somebody would have to shinny up the price marquee and quickly lower our price to 11.9. Those were the days of gasoline price wars because there was too much gasoline. We won't ever have those wars again.

There should be a global price for retail gasoline. Wholesale gasoline is marketed just like oil. Retail gasoline is affected by politics—either through taxes or subsidies—so gasoline has differ-ent prices in different parts of the world. If you're in China, you're paying $2 a gallon; if you're in the United Kingdom, you're paying $9; if you're in the United States, you're paying $3.50 (or consider-ably more by the time this book goes to press). This sends confus-ing messages to consumers around the world: *If the price is low, the oil supply must be plentiful.* Until we have a clear message— which is, of course, supply is tight—at the retail level, you're not going to be able to control the demand for gasoline. You're going to control the demand for gasoline only one way: with price. We have to stop sleepwalking through the Peak Oil crisis and get real.

How?

Creativity.

Since the 1970s, every presidential candidate, Democrat or Republican, has said without hesitation, "If you elect me, we're going to become energy independent."

I've never seen anyone stand up and say, "Hold, it, pal. Explain how we're going to become energy independent."

The truth is, no one can say how it can happen . . . yet. All that is certain is this: as dependence on foreign oil continues to increase, the door will open wider to every conceivable alternative. Every alternative will have a chance now. New ideas once thought unfathomable always become more feasible when the price of a commodity gets high enough to make a profit on the alternative. What follows are four options currently being explored and, to varying degrees, utilized as unconventional oil sources.

CANADIAN OIL SANDS

One bright spot on the horizon is the oil sands in Canada, which *Time* described as that country's "greatest buried treasure." The oil sands are nothing new. I was living in Canada in 1967 when the Great Canadian Oil Sands, now Suncor, launched the first project to produce synthetic crude oil from oil sands in Fort McMurray, Alberta. Oil sands, a huge deposit of oil at or near the surface in Alberta, have long been touted as the key to meeting future demand for oil. One unique aspect of this oil is that it is mined, not drilled. The upgrading process yields very high quality oil. There's no question that there's a lot of oil in the sand. In 1967 I was thirty-nine years old. At the end of the day I'd occasionally stop by the Petroleum Club. Five or six of my fellow geologists would be there talking shop. I remember the night the Great Canadian Oil Sands operation was announced. We were all sitting around having a beer. It was a government project, and we all scoffed at the idea. There was just no way for it to make any money.

"You know, Boone, for this thing to work, you'd have to have five-dollar-a-barrel oil!" my good friend Harley Hotchkiss, the Canadian oilman and geologist, would say. We'd both laugh. The price of oil was $2.20 a barrel back then. We never imagined we'd see five-dollar-a-barrel oil. When oil hit $40 a barrel, oil sands not only made sense, they made billions—and turned Fort McMurray into a boomtown. The Alberta oil sands contain 250 billion barrels of oil, which are mined and then hauled by seven-million-dollar, two-story-high trucks that carry 400-ton payloads.

Suncor is the largest Canadian oil sands operator. At BP Capital, the oil sands is one of our biggest investments, one we've been in since 2001. Another production company thinking creatively and getting good results is Denbury, which is injecting carbon dioxide into depleted oil fields to enhance production. Denbury also owns the Jackson Dome in Mississippi, which has an estimated 13 trillion cubic feet of carbon dioxide.

Speaking of investments, don't overlook the major American oil companies just because they are in liquidation mode. They may not be able to replace their oil reserves, but this doesn't mean they aren't good investments. The majors will always be a decent investment. However, given their peaking reserve base and declining production numbers, the primary upside will be the development of their downstream operations coupled with the rising price of oil. Not necessarily the first place I'd go with my money, but it shouldn't be overlooked.

COAL TO LIQUID FUEL

The chief advantage of coal in the United States is that it's plentiful. It's been estimated that the United States has more than 250 billion tons of recoverable coal reserves—equivalent to 800 billion barrels of oil. Coal already provides more than half of America's electricity. New technology to convert coal into synthetic oil and oil products at a cost of approximately $35 per barrel is becoming attractive. The leader in the production of coal-to-liquids (CTL) is

Sasol, a South African company that produces 150,000 barrels of liquid fuel from coal per day. The company produced the first sample of synthetic oil from coal at its plant near Johannesburg in 1955. Since then, Sasol has produced almost 1.5 billion barrels of synthetic fuel and presently supplies about 28 percent of South Africa's fuel needs from coal. Yet coal is, and will continue to be, a double-edged sword. It's very important because we have so much of it, but coal is environmentally problematic because of emissions. To clean up coal as much as needed, you lose the cheap end of the deal.

INCREASED DEEPWATER PRODUCTION

Yes, there are offshore basins for oil exploration, but there hasn't been a big oil field found offshore in the deepwater Gulf of Mexico since 1999. There is deepwater exploration happening around the world. Current technologies allow us to drill wells that we never thought were possible. The Tupi discovery in Brazil, for example, is in seven thousand feet of water and is located below a thick layer of salt. The discovery was estimated to cost over $200 million. So I think there is still potential for deepwater discoveries. However, what we find in the remainder of the outer continental shelf around the world will not do anything more than repace declining production.

These days we're not finding billion-barrel discoveries that can be brought on line quickly. Rather, we're finding a few 100-million-barrel fields that can be brought on line in five to ten years. So what are we going to do for the next decade? It's yet another confirmation of the predicament we find ourselves in.

OIL SHALE

In 2006, Shell and Chevron were granted leases to extract oil from shale in western Colorado. A long and complicated process is required to remove oil from rock, but the idea is by no means new. According to Shell's website dedicated to its oil shale project:

> Ute Indian legends told of warriors who saw lightning hit certain rock formations causing the "rocks to burn." There is even a story of a Parachute [Colorado] area rancher who built a rock fireplace in his new cabin. When the first flames heated the fireplace, the chimney, primarily com- posed of oil shale, caught fire and burnt the entire struc- ture to the ground. Pioneers in the western United States fueled their campfires with shale and used its oily residue to grease their wagon axles. Shale also was used as a fuel to heat peach orchards during winters in Palisade.

In the 1980s, the major U.S. oil companies invested billions to attempt to produce oil from shale. When the price of oil collapsed in 1985, they walked away from these projects. I've seen estimates that U.S. oil shale reserves could contain 1.5 trillion barrels of oil, five times the stated reserves of Saudi Arabia. I hope this turns out to be true. I don't know much about oil shale, except that I'll be long gone before they produce oil from shale in meaningful amounts.

THE AGE OF ALTERNATIVES MUST BEGIN IMMEDIATELY

Here's the truth about alternatives: we're going to need all of them. With supply pushed to the brink by unquenchable demand, we're going to need everything. We're going to need all of the oil and gas we can find. We're going to need ethanol, natural gas, solar, wind, biofuels, and nuclear. In an energy-starved world, our country is the hungriest. We're going to need invention, breakthroughs, new sources of energy for power and fuel. A premium will go to environmentally friendly fuels.

In 2007, I was invited to speak at the thirteenth annual Alternative Fuels and Vehicles National Conference in Anaheim, California. It is the premier conference on alternative fuels, vehicles, and advanced technologies. The first time I attended ten years ago, two hundred people were there. In 2007, there were fifteen hundred, along with every conceivable alternative-fuel vehicle.

"I don't see a competitor in this room," I told the audience. All of us can be for one anothers' projects. What matters most is helping America, as well as making a profit. All of us are in this together, and now is the time to cooperate. Being environmentally conscious is in vogue these days, but I've been green all my life. When I would go bird hunting with my dad in Holdenville, we'd drive down the highway toward the Seminole oil field, which was twenty miles from our house. When we got near the field, I could see dead trees along the creek. "What's happening to the trees, Dad?" I asked. He explained that the oil company was dumping salt water into the creek, and it was killing all the trees. I don't know why that made such an impression on me, but it did. Here was this beautiful creek, and all along it were these dead trees. While global warming is hard to sell to a geologist, I believe we have to take it seriously. There is more than enough evidence in the shrinkage of the ice caps, which have been stable for thousands of years. We have to deal with this.

What harm is there in assuming that global warming is happening—and fast? Although it might cost more, what could be bad about reducing our energy consumption, pollution, and our carbon footprint? There's no downside, so you might as well do it. What comes out of it? We'll all adopt better practices as individuals, from a corporate standpoint and as a society. We'll be more sensitive to air quality and pollution than we've ever been before, and I think that's good. The additional cost will not be wasted.

"Our reliance on oil hangs over our country like a sword," I told the audience at the convention. Something needs to be done, and that something is alternatives. Like oil sands and CTL, many alternatives to conventional oil production were once considered too expensive. Today they are looking affordable. It's all driven by economics. You will see more wind energy now that producers can make a profit from it. Nobody will put up the billions required to produce wind energy if it is not profitable.

This upside potential is one of the reasons Texas has replaced California as the nation's wind energy leader. In 1999, Governor George W. Bush signed into law a bill that deregulated electric utilities in the Lone Star State. Less than a decade later, this nascent power source has blossomed. According to the American Wind Energy Association, Texas is now home to four of the nation's five largest wind farms. In 2007, 2 percent of the state's total electricity was generated by wind power, and that percentage is going up fast.

In 2007, President Bush said that by 2017 we'll need 35 billion gallons of alternative fuel per year to reduce our dependence on foreign oil. Where are we going to get these alternatives? Here are a few possibilities.

NATURAL GAS

This is the fuel of the future. It's our second-largest natural resource, next to coal. I've been a big believer in natural gas since the 1980s, when I started trying to sell it as a transportation fuel. I had my own motives for it; I had bet my company, Mesa, on my belief that natural gas prices were going to rise. Not only is natural gas a premium fuel but it also produces at least 75 percent fewer smog-forming chemicals than gasoline and 83 percent fewer than diesel. It's also cheaper and domestically produced, and our reserves are increasing annually.

Back in the 1980s, I was thinking, *If I can get natural gas over to transportation, I'll be home free.* Although it didn't happen back then, I'm convinced it's going to happen now. In those days, when I'd get up in front of an audience and say, "Natural gas is cleaner, cheaper, and a domestic fuel," the only bell that would ring was "cheaper." Today, with foreign oil imports becoming a global powder keg, the word "domestic" rings the loudest. So let's move natural gas from power generation to transportation; it's the highest-priced fuel in the United States when used for power generation, but it's cheaper than gasoline or diesel when used for transportation. Natural gas is too valuable to use for power generation. You're taking a better fuel and making something less out of it. It should become the second infrastructure alongside gasoline and diesel. If you believe that foreign oil will be the benchmark for fossil fuels, as I do, then natural gas will never sell at a price higher than gasoline and diesel.

As I've said before, some alternatives are better suited than others. For example, ethanol is really a blend, a "stretcher" for gasoline. It also is a light-duty fuel that cannot be used in a heavy-duty engine. Biodiesel works, but it's more expensive and somewhat limited—especially considering some estimates that we will be able to produce only 2 billion gallons by 2015. Biodiesel is also dirtier than natural gas or ethanol and has to be blended with diesel.

The United States uses 175 billion gallons of gasoline and diesel combined each year. If the current 7 Tcf (trillion cubic feet) of natural gas we're using each year for power generation were utilized for transportation purposes, it would represent a reduction of

38 percent of our foreign imports. This is a substantially larger amount than I have seen anybody else come up with.

The natural gas fueling company I founded, Clean Energy Fuels (NASDAQ: CLNE), has 190 fueling stations and is projecting an additional 45 new stations per year. I know it has a real future, and the market is moving our way. Worldwide there were 7 million natural gas vehicles on the road in 2007, yet only 150,000 of those were in the United States. This is another example of the leadership vacuum crippling this country. The major oil companies and Big Three automakers have quashed this initiative, so we're behind everyone else once again. Natural gas is a superior alternative, and it's time for us to catch up with the rest of the world. Remember, it is our second most plentiful natural resource, and we import only a small percentage.

ELECTRIC/HYBRID

Although the hybrid cars on the road today are getting considerable attention and increased sales, the electric car hasn't happened yet despite a considerable investment by California. I once served on an energy commission appointed by President Clinton. All of the alternative fuels were represented. An electric-car proponent was expounding the virtues of electric cars. He said he had "rigged up" a booster, which he towed in a trailer behind his electric car. With the additional power, his car could "zoom" over hills at more than "35 miles an hour!" I loved the story and asked the guy if he would travel with me and tell his story at our presentations for natural gas vehicles. I knew then and now that natural-gas-powered vehicles are much more practical.

When I gave speeches in California a decade ago, someone would stand up and ask, "What do you think about the electric car,

Boone?" I'd reply, "Does anyone know where the electricity will come from to power all of the electric cars?" Most people would point to a wall socket. "Is the source of that power natural gas, nuclear, coal, or hydroelectric?" I'd ask. Nobody had an answer back then. The power has to come from somewhere, and it isn't cheap.

ETHANOL

Whoever convinced President Bush that ethanol is a viable alternative is one hell of a good salesman. Ethanol is a bit of a dilemma to me. Shifting corn from a foodstuff to a fuel source makes farmers more money, but it also costs consumers more at the grocery store. It is not a long-term solution.

Having said that, will ethanol work? Yes.

Is it cleaner than gasoline? No.

Does it have the same power as gasoline? No, only 70 percent of the power.

Will it work for your car? Yes, it will.

In 1988, I was not a believer in ethanol, but a lot of things have changed since then, including our $1 trillion addiction to imported oil. I am somewhat of a believer now. We're getting close to 1 million barrels a day in ethanol production, and that amount will replace a small percentage of the oil we import.

It costs a lot of money to produce ethanol, and the process has to be subsidized to make it economically feasible for the producer. That said, I would rather subsidize ethanol than buy oil from people who don't like us. Whatever fuel we can produce at home is better than what we have to buy from abroad. It creates jobs here. It produces taxes here. It doesn't go out the back door, never to be seen again. I'd damn near rather use anything other than foreign oil, be it wood chips, switchgrass, or wadded-up newspapers.

In the late 1980s, I was in a meeting with half a dozen senators when I expressed my doubts about ethanol. I couldn't believe the U.S. government was subsidizing a fuel that actually costs more than it's worth. Afterward, my good friend Senator Bob Dole took me out into the hall.

"People up here aren't stupid," the Kansas senator told me. "They understand what you're saying, and you're wasting your time telling them something they already know."

"OK, what else?" I asked.

"There are twenty-one farm states in the United States, and they have forty-two senators, and they're all together on ethanol," he said. "So don't think you're going to explain to us that we don't need to subsidize ethanol."

"OK, I understand. We're going to have ethanol."

But just because I understood the politics of ethanol didn't make it a good fuel. Still, if you planted a cornfield from the Mississippi River to the Pacific Ocean and took all of the corn and made ethanol out of it, that would be about 17 billion gallons, half of the alternative fuel the president says we'll need. With all the corn that is currently planted in the United States, ethanol supplies almost 5 percent of our transportation fuel. Do I like ethanol? It's our ugly baby, and I like it a hell of a lot better than imported oil. But we need to get on cellulosic ethanol—biofuel made from switchgrass, wood chips, and other plant mass—as quick as we can and get corn back in supermarkets, not gas stations. This can be accomplished with the right leadership in Washington supporting the right incentives.

SOLAR

I used to wonder when the price would get right for solar. Thanks to $100 oil, I think the price must be getting very close despite the rising costs of silicon, a key material in solar panels. The potential for solar power is great. *Scientific American* estimated that solar power could produce five thousand times the electricity currently consumed in the world. As far as solar for transportation goes, I can't see widespread use of solar for powering vehicles—at least not in the near future. Although we're not there yet, the day for solar is coming fast.

WE'RE CONSTANTLY STUDYING new ideas at BP Capital. One day we were looking at a deal for converting gas to liquids and another plan to convert coal to liquids. When we were finished with our analysis, Alex Szewczyk, who runs our equity fund, asked, "Do you think these deals are going to work?"

"Yes, all of them work," I said. "Your job isn't finding out what will work. Because of my age, you have to find the ones that work first."

I'm certain that I will never wait in line at a red light behind a hydrogen-powered car. The technology is decades away. The fuel is not a natural resource and has to be manufactured, which makes it cost-prohibitive. Biofuels? Some day. In my lifetime, biofuels probably won't cover a significant percentage of the alternatives. But what I will see and what you are seeing today is how the effects of Peak Oil are making alternative fuel sources and costly technologies far more viable in today's marketplace.

CHAPTER 8

Going Long and Scoring Big

Booneism #19: *We're catching 'em faster than we can string 'em.*

WITH CHALLENGE COMES opportunity. There are still going to be opportunities for the producer and the investor in the oil business. However, it's not the same oil business that it was when I got into it in 1940, pumping gas for 11 cents a gallon at Ray Smith's Sinclair station in Holdenville. And it's worlds away from the oil business that my dad got into in 1923. In the decades since, the oil business has changed several times, and the next one will be a dramatic one. There's no question that if you can change with it, if you can understand and follow the fundamentals, you can still make a lot of money in oil and gas, which is exactly what we did on an unprecedented level in late 2004 and early 2005.

Every commodity is governed by the forces of supply and demand. If you grow more corn, the price goes down. When corn is in short supply, the price goes up. When we analyzed the oil and gas futures markets in the spring of 2003, supply was the strongest indicator of future pricing. And it was clear that the biggest influences on supply were going to include the war in Iraq, unrest in the Middle East, and uncertainty in Nigeria and Venezuela.

On March 2, a *New York Times* headline read "Jump in Price of Oil Puts New Strains on Economy." The story read:

> The potential war in the Persian Gulf, political chaos in Venezuela, and a cold winter in the United States caused the price of a barrel of oil to soar to almost $40 on Thursday, the highest since Iraq invaded Kuwait in 1990, before it retreated to $36.60 on Friday in New York. That is up about 69 percent from a year ago.

Immediately following the U.S. invasion of Iraq on March 19, the price of oil slid to $26. There had been a steep run-up in oil prices in anticipation of the war. By the time the invasion came, it was anticlimactic—at least as it affected the price of oil. If you'd asked someone before the invasion, "Why are you buying oil?" the answer would likely have been, "Because we are about to invade Iraq." After the invasion, that reason was gone and the price went down. The same thing happened in 1991 in the first Gulf War. The price of oil went up before the invasion, then collapsed the week afterward.

By May oil futures were trading at about $30 a barrel, a low price considering how much it costs to find and produce oil. I knew that was too cheap. I was convinced that Iraq's production after the invasion was not going to recover as quickly as most thought. When we invaded, Iraq's oil production was between 2.5 million and 3 million barrels of oil a day. After the invasion, it dropped to almost zero. Over time it has slowly inched back up to 2 million barrels a day.

Consider my three rules of energy:

No. 1: The cost of finding oil and gas is always higher than you originally think.

No. 2: Oil and gas always take longer than expected to get on production.

No. 3: Discoveries are never as large as producers originally think.

Think of a tennis ball and how it bounces: the first bounce is the highest. Your initial discovery of oil and gas on day one is like the first bounce. As you learn more about the discovery and actually start to produce, you'll usually find that estimates of the reserves "bounced" better on day one. More often than not you're disappointed by subsequent estimates. That's the nature of this game.

These rules held true for Iraq in the spring of 2003. When you knock out an entire OPEC nation's production, it's not going to bounce back fast. With production down and demand rising, there was only one direction for oil prices to go: UP.

We had been long oil since the fall of 2002, so we understood that there were factors other than the impending invasion of Iraq. The world economy was growing after a slight recession in 2001. Plagued by accounting scandals and weak profit reports, the stock market had fallen for three years in a row. The stock market had a huge year in 2003, with the S&P up 40 percent from May 2003 lows.

Two of our indicators signaled that we should be buying oil: the growing economy and the likelihood that Iraqi production would be slowed for a long time. By December 2003, nine months after the invasion, the price of oil hit $30 a barrel. There was talk of a "terrorist premium," a $5 to $10 per barrel extra cost that I found no basis for. There was never any terrorist premium. It was just the market. By this time the conventional wisdom was that oil prices had already topped out. The thinking went, *The price of oil should be $20, and it's now $30. That's 50 percent higher than it was just six months ago. It can't go much higher than $30. You're going to kill demand.*

That's what most people thought. I disagreed, and I still don't know how high it has to go before you kill demand. After the price of oil reached a low of $26 a barrel in May 2003, it went up to $33 by the end of the year, and I still wanted to buy more oil. Not only was conventional wisdom against that, but at times my own team wasn't convinced. Yet the fundamentals pointed to an even bigger rise. So if oil was down a dollar, I'd tell my guys, "We should be buying the pull-backs."

By May 2004, oil had gone from $30 to $40, a gain of $10 in the first five months of the year. Again, conventional wisdom was screaming to get out of the market. *"The price is too high! You're going to kill demand, and the price is going to fall back to $20!"* Yet the price kept moving higher: $30, then $40, then $50. The price would reach a level where it would briefly impact demand, and then demand would go up again.

By this time we had begun one of the best plays in our history. Opportunities of this magnitude are not like streetcars. They don't come by every fifteen minutes. They come by every few years. The key is to spot them, get on board, and don't be quick to get off. Stick with it.

By the time the price hit $40 a barrel that May, something of major importance was becoming clear to us. It was an indicator of very big things to come. It was as simple as this: producers should have reacted by increasing production. If you're a producer and you watch the price go from $28 to $40 in a year, what are you going to do? You're going to take your oil to market as fast as possible. It's a case of economics. Whether you produced in West Texas or in one of the thirteen OPEC nations, the time to sell your oil would have been then. The price of oil had just shot up 60 percent.

The odd thing was we didn't see an increase in oil production; only stronger demand. Worldwide demand was growing by more than 3.5 million barrels a day; 2004 saw the largest one-year jump in demand in twenty years. People called it "demand shock." This was a very different scenario from the "oil shock" of 1980, when the price of oil soared after the Iranian revolution and then slid down a year or so later. There was plenty of oil back then. This was more a question of supply. The demand shock was not temporary. It was permanent, owing mainly to economic growth in China and India. Every barrel of oil being produced was being claimed. China added as much demand as the United States. India added as much as Europe. This resulted in wild fluctuations in oil prices.

Why was there no corresponding jump in production? That was the question we asked in our Investment Committee meetings that went on morning, noon, and night. We kept looking at the fundamentals. Demand was rocketing higher, and there was no major supply response despite a 60 percent rise in price. Something had to be happening to keep production from soaring.

Supply response is easy to see. Oil companies love to draw attention to discoveries, especially big ones. If a company makes a big discovery or puts more production on line, they trumpet the news to the street. In this case, there were some minor increases in oil production but not nearly as much as you would expect given the price increase.

We went through $40 oil like a hot knife through butter. In

October 2004, the price hit $50 a barrel. Still there was no supply response. Either OPEC had the oil and wanted to keep the price high, or, even worse, they didn't have it. I voted that they didn't have it, and I was very much in the minority. My confidence level was coming up. If we didn't have a supply response by $50, we knew the price was going to go higher. That's when the alarm began ringing. There was only one reason that the oil flow was not meeting demand at that price, and it was something that had been predicted back in 1956: Peak Oil.

We bought oil futures throughout the remainder of 2004 and into 2005. We might have been in Dallas, but our fingers were on the pulse of oil markets worldwide. We were about to reap the biggest rewards of our business careers. By now I felt so confident that the price of oil was going up, I wasn't hesitant to voice my predictions publicly.

In May 2004, when oil was just above $40, I went on CNBC and predicted that the price of oil would soon surpass $50 a barrel. By September, when oil was near $50, I said in a radio interview, "I think you're going to see sixty dollars before you see forty dollars!" In December, when oil futures were at $55, I told Bloomberg News that prices would reach $60 by the early part of the following year. I was right on every count. It wasn't magic, but it sure looked like magic. It was simple tracking of supply and demand.

It was clear that oil prices were headed up, and this opened up an enormous window of opportunity. We were holding between 20,000 and 40,000 futures contracts. Each contract is 1,000 barrels, which meant our position ranged from 20 to 40 million barrels of oil. At $45 a barrel, these contracts represented a value of about $1.3 billion. Most of our contracts were three or four months out.

Once a contract matured, we would roll it out for a longer period. We were constantly rolling our contracts, betting our conviction that the price of oil would continue to rise. With robust worldwide demand and a strained supply, what else could the price do? Yet in the middle of all this, if you looked at the forward price curve—in 2004, in 2005, and in 2006—it was a descending line. The price didn't go up. Instead, the price went down. The market was saying that in the future, oil would become cheaper, not more expensive.

For instance, in June 2004, the spot price of oil was $37 a barrel. Five years out, the price was $30 a barrel. This is what traders refer to as a backwardated market. To us it represented an enormous opportunity. There was no way oil could go down, and the odds of it moving up were almost assured. It was a 10/1 bet, and we put the chips on the table.

It set up our 2005 oil play. We needed to be long. Very long. We began buying the back of the oil futures curve, purchasing oil five and ten years out. Brokers were making markets for us that didn't exist, because, again, few people had ever wanted to buy oil that far out.

"As long as they're giving it to us, we've got to keep taking it," I told my guys.

Then in the summer of 2005 Hurricanes Katrina and Rita tore into the Gulf and shut down all production. The price shot up above $70 before dropping to $61 by year's end. That was still 40 percent higher than on the final day of trading in 2004. Analysts were cautioning that production limits and rising demand would lead to higher prices in 2006.

Everyone saw what we had seen in the commodity curve. A year later the front of the market was at $60 and the back was at $60, a flat line all the way. The price of oil at the front of the curve had gone up by $25, while the back had gone up by $30. By 2007, the current month's oil price was $75 a barrel, and the back of the market, 10 years out, was $68. We had gone into backwardation on the curve, and the distant years were very attractive as long as we believed that demand would rise and supply would be no better than 85 million barrels a day.

> **Booneism #20:** *I find that the more generous I am, the more I get in return, and the more I get in return, the more generous I am.*

OUR FUNDS CAME out of 2005 with huge profits. That year represented the biggest move in the price of oil in the previous twenty years. Thank God we were on board and had the boat loaded. The price went from about $30 in the first quarter of 2004 to above $70 in August 2005. By the end of the year, we had made $405 million on oil futures. Coupled with our natural gas trades, the BP Capital Energy Fund was up $1.3 billion for the year, 248 percent after fees. The BP Capital Energy Equity Fund had equally impressive results in 2005: up $532 million, or 89 percent after fees.

Our Investment Committee meeting was held at Al Biernat's just before Christmas 2005. That year I got to play Santa Claus. Before I began to distribute $50 million in bonuses to our team, I had several things to say.

"I'm getting ready to pass out a lot of money, and I want you to remember a few things," I began. "First, don't be foolish with the money you've made. No big cars. Second, remember who you are. Stay humble and be generous. It's the right thing to do, and it feels good."

I have a lot of young guys on my team. I think it's important they learn that lesson sooner rather than later. I take that advice to heart, and they know I do. I play it out every day. Giving to worthy causes is something I've done throughout my lifetime. In the last days of 2005, I stepped it up. When I'm making money, I'm easy Pickens for a good cause.

CHAPTER 9

Stepping Up My Giving

Booneism #21: I love making money. But I also love giving it away. Not as much as making it, but it's a very close second.

I BELIEVE I was put on this earth to make money and be generous with it. Once I made a billion dollars, I knew I had to be giving more of it away. Throughout my life, I've given away close to 2 billion dollars to a wide range of causes, including health and medical research and services, entrepreneurship, kids at risk, education and athletics, and conservation and wildlife management initiatives. Many of the donations involved millions of dollars and attracted headlines; others were equally important but less heralded.

A few years ago I decided to step up my philanthropy in a major way, not just in the number of causes and dollars but in an even more ambitious manner. At my age, a dollar saved is a dollar wasted. I decided I didn't want to wait until after I was dead to give away my fortune; I wanted to see the impact of my donations in my lifetime.

Some of my giving is personal. I've supported research that advances our understanding of the brain. Autism, Alzheimer's, cancer—these are some of the challenges that are being studied, and it matters a great deal to me because I lost my mother to an inoperable brain tumor.

Aside from the good giving does for others, it does a lot of good for oneself. Giving is another form of engagement, of staying active and involved in the world outside of the office. Our giving is donor-directed. We're participatory, interested, involved, and proactive. We know where we want to make a difference. We find people that have the leadership skills and the capability to make a difference, and we fund them. We're always looking for leadership. We like results and want to ensure that the individuals, entities, and organizations we support are doing what they said they were going to do. When we find someone who is doing a good job, we consider them a client of ours instead of us being a client of theirs.

In December 2006, the numbers had gotten so large that I decided not only to give personally but also to create a new giving structure: The T. Boone Pickens Foundation. I seeded the foundation with an initial $135 million gift. My mandate was to spend it all within a year and replenish it at year's end. The board members are Ron Bassett, Andrew Littlefair, Bobby Stillwell, and me. It was starting a new business, one of the most exciting ventures I've ever launched—the business of giving and helping. Interestingly, it was funded with more money than any other business that I ever started, and for the first time it was only my money. There were no outside investors or partners.

My philanthropic approach is not unlike my business approach. I don't plant small trees. Why? Because of my age. I'm not out to change an organization for a day or a month. I'm out to change the lives of as many people as possible.

Shortly before launching the foundation, I hired Marti Carlin to look at the hundreds and even thousands of organizations seeking our support. The requests come in a variety of ways: from a friend of a friend, a formal proposal, a handwritten letter, an audience member at a speech, or a media appearance. There is no shortage of need in the world. Our job is to determine which organizations will help the greatest number of people and do the greatest good. When presented with a new cause, I'll say, "Put the bird dog on it," referring to Marti. We go to work, meeting the principals, visiting their facilities, and studying the findings.

My parents were frugal, but they would always help people who would help themselves. My grandfather was a Methodist minister, and I was brought up in the church. I believe I was put on this earth to help people. Consequently, I believe I'm doing what the Lord wants me to do.

This was ingrained in me early on. When I was a kid in Holdenville, the local Red Cross would distribute red crosses on cards for donors to hang in their front windows. My grandmother's house was one of two on the block to display this cross. The other was my folks'.

I was seven when I asked how she got it.

"Because we contributed. We help the Red Cross by giving them money."

It wasn't much money—probably only a dollar or two. She always gave, and every year she had a cross in her window.

"Why doesn't everyone have a cross in their window?" I asked her.

"Because everybody doesn't give," she said.

The Frisco and the Rock Island rail lines crossed in Holdenville, so you had rail traffic with guys who hitched rides on the trains. They would get off and walk down the street looking for something to eat. We lived three blocks from the railroad. Guys would come to our house and ask for food.

"I'll feed you if you'll work while I'm fixing your food," my grandmother would tell them. "It'll probably be an hour until your food is ready."

The boxcar bum would carry out the trash, clean the yard, whatever my grandmother wanted. An hour or so later, after eating a hot meal, he'd leave. Some were better than others. What those guys did was probably mark her house in some way. Another guy would come along. Then another. Until finally my grandmother said, "I must be marked somehow. They always come to me."

When I'm expected to do something, I always want to do more. Whether it's a one-night auction or a fund-raising campaign, I always push it to the limit. Let me give you an example. I'm competitive. At my age, people love to give me awards, usually at luncheons or dinners. All are set up as fund-raisers. They call me a legend. That goes along with the pitch. Every time I'm approached to participate in one of these events, I ask the same question: "What's your previous record, and how can we beat it?" I want to beat the record and in the process help the organization set a new bar for subsequent events that create even greater value for the cause.

Some gifts extend beyond a lifetime, which is the case with my single biggest gift: $165 million to Oklahoma State University's athletic department. The original amount has now grown to over $300 million. It's the largest gift ever made to college athletics in the

United States. But that's only temporary. Somebody will top it. When the donation was announced in January 2006, the media had one question: Why would you give such a large gift to athletics and not academics? Why? Because I wanted to. Actually, it goes much deeper than that. I have a strategic plan.

Two years after my $165-million gift to the OSU athletic department, I followed it up with a $100-million academic gift. I'm counting on OSU president Burns Hargis to raise another $100 million in response. That combined $200 million will be eligible for a dollar-for-dollar match through the State of Oklahoma's endowed chair program, and with that leverage my $100-million gift will become $400 million. When you combine my earlier donations, the proceeds from the two Gifts of a Lifetime (which I discuss later in this chapter), and the investment income that's been earned, I've achieved my strategic plan of raising well over $1 billion for Oklahoma State. Do you suppose I can make it to $2 billion?

OSU is where I went to college. I gave the money because I'm competitive. I don't like losing. And OSU's football team was doing just that. They didn't have the resources to be competitive in the Big 12. I wanted to fix that. I was embarrassed about the losses and how that reflected on the school. Once again, it was a leadership problem. It was now or never for OSU. I felt I had to do whatever I could to give the school a competitive edge. I understand we're not going to win every game, but I do expect to be competitive every game. OSU's missing link was money.

Now that I had it, I was willing to give it to the school. My gift would represent a rare opportunity not only for OSU but also for my goal of being able to see what good my money could do in my lifetime. At OSU, I am able to see the results on a scoreboard.

PICKENS GIVES OSU SOARING AMBITION
Tuesday, September 4, 2007
By CHIP BROWN
The Dallas Morning News

ATHENS, GA. — The wheels touch down five miles from the University of Georgia campus, and the first thing Dallas billionaire T. Boone Pickens sees after leaving the $50 million, leather-couch comfort of his Gulfstream 550 is a stuffed cowboy (for the OSU Cowboys) hanging from the control tower.

It's almost as if the Bulldogs knew Pickens was coming.

"This isn't Nebraska, where the fans applaud you if you win," Pickens says. "If we win, these Georgia fans are going to be nasty."

The day started with Pickens quickly bagging his limit of 15 doves while hunting with family and friends on his 68,000-acre ranch near Pampa in the Texas Panhandle.

All Pickens could talk about as he picked off birds as if they were stationary targets at a state fair was the Oklahoma State–Georgia game, set to kick off at 5:45 p.m. Central time.

"This is big," said Pickens, whose energy and stamina belie his 79 years. "We find out where we are tonight. The whole country may be talking about Oklahoma State tomorrow."

My wife, Madeleine, said that OSU has become my number one priority. I told her that I didn't think that was so. There's BP Capital and the various deals we have ongoing. But she said, "No, Boone. I know it's OSU because of how much you talk about it. You talk about OSU more than any other subject." I couldn't argue. After all, she's the one who has to listen.

For as long as I can remember, I have always placed a high value on victory in sports. In high school and college, basketball, not football, became the most important thing in my life. Long before I got to high school in 1943, I practiced shooting baskets in the backyard for hours at a time regardless of the season. I played in every pickup game that I could find. I dreamed of winning state championships and being carried off the court by my victorious teammates. I played guard for the Holdenville Wolverines and later earned a spot on my Amarillo High School team, the Golden Sandstorm. I was five feet nine inches tall, thanks in part to my grandmother cautioning me as a kid not to smoke or drink coffee. "It'll stunt your growth," she said. I'd often reflect back on that advice. "If you'd drunk coffee or smoked cigars, you might not have made it to five feet," my grandmother told me.

I was a starter for the Amarillo Sandies when we reached the semifinals at the 1947 state tournament. Thomas Jefferson High School of San Antonio was ranked number one in the state, led by Kyle Rote, an all-around athlete who'd go on to fame as an All-Pro running back with the New York Giants. The game came off as predicted: tighter than Dick's hat band. With thirty seconds left, we were up 37-36. The crowd was on its feet, rooting for the underdogs from Amarillo. I was inspired to play the best game of my life . . . until Kyle Rote knocked the ball out of my hand. I fouled him after he got the ball, and he got one free throw to tie the game. He missed, but Jefferson's center, Benny White, followed up with a tip-in for the winning basket. In the course of the game, I had made four shots outside the circle, but this was long before they counted as three points. If we had been playing today, we would have won with those three-pointers. Timing is everything. I was just forty years off. "Don't worry about it. You played a good game," our coach, T. G. Hull, told me afterward.

I thought I was good enough to land a college basketball scholarship. "Son, if you are as good as you think you are, they'll find you," my mother would tell me.

At the end of my senior year, I got my only scholarship offer: $25 a month from Texas A&M. When I arrived at College Station, somebody yelled down the hall, "Coach, got a basketball player checking in!" Coach Marty Karow came walking up.

"Hi, Coach, I'm Boone Pickens."

"Boone Pickens! Hell, I thought you were bigger!" His assistant had recruited me.

"Well, I've lost three pounds. I've had my wisdom teeth pulled."

"I meant I thought you were taller."

I made the freshman team, but I can't say I was a standout. Sometime during the season I realized that after I'd made the varsity I'd be one of the players who'd get to play the last two minutes if we were up by ten or down by ten. My basketball days at A&M appeared even shorter when I realized they weren't going to renew my scholarship. Looking back, I laugh about that even more after reading a story in a Texas A&M publication in 2007 called *The 12th Man*. They did a piece on the ten biggest mistakes the Aggies ever made. High on the list was "The year they cut Boone Pickens off a $25-a-month scholarship." Bobby Farmer, my old high school friend who played for the Aggies, told me, "Well, Pick, if you'd have stayed at A&M, maybe you could have really made something of yourself."

I had gone to A&M to become a veterinarian. When it was clear my scholarship wasn't going to be renewed, I looked for a school that would accept my agriculture hours. Sometimes I think the Lord directed me to Oklahoma A&M, now called Oklahoma State University, in Stillwater. My ag credits transferred to OSU, and off I went. The legendary OSU coach Henry Iba told me I could walk on. In two months, I was a walk-on and a walk-off. I was finished with basketball. It was out of my system. I wasn't going to get any taller and I wasn't going to get any faster. It was time for me to exit the arena and get serious about college.

After going through rush, I pledged my father's fraternity, Sigma Alpha Epsilon, and my father came to Stillwater in February 1949 for the initiation ceremony. He used the same pin he received when he was at Cumberland University in Tennessee in 1921. Afterward he said something that changed the direction of my life.

"Your mother and I have something we want you to know," he said.

I knew that invoking the name of my mother meant that this was serious.

"We think you're wasting your time," he said. "You're not getting anywhere."

I had to admit I wasn't burning up the place.

"What do you think I should do?"

"Get in geology and graduate in June 1951."

I knew he was right. A month after Dad's visit, I switched my major to geology, and I got married. I made the dean's list and graduated on time.

When I graduated, Dad said, "Son, I'm proud of you. You got out on time. I have one more thing for you." I was sure he was going to give me some money. Somehow I had in my head it was $300. Sure enough, he stuck out his hand. No envelope, but a warm handshake. "Good luck" was all he said. What a deal. Here I was. I had graduated. I had a great upbringing. I had a good education. I didn't owe a dime. I had a family. I had every reason to go out and be successful. Off I went to Bartlesville, Oklahoma, to work for Phillips. I was on my way.

I needed OSU back then, and once I made a billion dollars, OSU needed me. Again, it was most unusual that I even wound up going to college there and would leave with such a strong affinity for the school. If I had gone to Texas A&M or the University of Texas — major state schools with large numbers of wealthy alumni — I could never have had the impact that I'm having at OSU today. Impact meaning what? That the money I have given can help the school become competitive in both athletics *and* academics.

OSU has won forty-eight NCAA national championships over the years. That's the fourth-highest number of any college in NCAA history. We've had some great basketball teams and were the first school to win back-to-back national championships in 1945 and 1946. But that was a long time ago. We've won ten NCAA crowns in golf and thirty-four in wrestling. But in more recent years the OSU football team has struggled with glimmers of hope followed by long periods of total frustration. Even when the team performed well it couldn't sustain the momentum in a tough conference dominated by powerhouses such as Nebraska, Oklahoma, and Texas. Our 1987 football team had two great running backs — Barry Sanders and Thurman Thomas. Both went on to pro careers and the NFL Hall of Fame, the first time in history that two players in the same college backfield became Hall of Famers. That could have been something to build a future on. Instead, it was a prelude to a scandal.

In 1989, the NCAA Committee on Infractions punished OSU with four years' probation for more than forty recruiting violations, including the purchase of cars and payments to football players. All

were by boosters. This made me sick, but I can't say I was surprised.
I had been approached by one of the assistant coaches.

"You know all the schools are cheating," he began. It was soon
evident he was telling me about a slush fund of some sort operating outside the athletic department.

"Hold it," I said. "When I give, every check will be made out to
the OSU Athletic Department and marked for golf, football, basketball, or whatever."

When the NCAA investigation began, I never got one call. That's
not the way you win. After the sanctions, upgrades to the athletic
program virtually stopped. From 1967 to 1987, OSU spent $11.7
million on facilities. From 1987 until 1999, the school invested
nothing, and the performance of the university teams was what one
might have guessed, considering the deteriorating situation.

The football wasn't a disaster—from 1997 to 2002, we beat OU
five times in eight years. It was our best stretch ever, and we're
counting on bringing those days back. But our stadium was pitiful.
It was falling down. Lewis Field had been nicknamed "Rustoleum
Stadium" by our archrivals, who liked to add that it was located in
Stoolwater. The stadium looked like it had never been painted and
had been taken over by the rust worms. In Texas it wouldn't have
even qualified as a middle-of-the-road high school stadium.

Just as I believe that no human being should allow himself to be
sidelined because of age, I believe that an underdog like OSU
should have the chance to become competitive. That's the key
word: *competitive.* Soon after, the key word becomes *win,* and
that's where we are today: WIN.

This goal has become a very big part of my life. My wife may be
right about it being my priority. Sports aren't the primary thing a university is about. I also want to make OSU competitive academically.

But building a school's athletic department helps it rise above mediocrity and attain a level of confidence and self-esteem. Winning in sports brings more students and more funds, which benefits the entire university. Winning is contagious.

Larry Reece, OSU's executive director of development and major gifts, says that athletics is "the front porch of the university. That's how you advertise nationally." A winning sports program builds a university's brand nationally as well as internationally. "Right, wrong, or indifferent, you don't see the Science Bowl on ABC. You see the Cotton Bowl and the Final Four."

You don't get fifty thousand people to go to a stadium to listen to a history professor; that doesn't grab the attention of the masses. Football is big in America, and a school with a competitive college football program will attract more students, which attracts better teachers, and in turn leads to academic greatness. We're building the best facilities in America for college sports. I want a great university, and a competitive sports program is a way to get there.

Funding and leadership make a difference. If you can provide the funding and attract the leadership, you can win. I didn't donate the money to buy a winning football team. You can't buy victory. It goes deeper than dollars and cents. But money is a good place to start.

In business I always see myself as an underdog. I love that position, especially when I'm able to prove people wrong when they say, "You can't make that deal," or "You can't win that game." In OSU, I saw another underdog.

Booneism #22: That deal where you throw the ball and then run down the field and catch the ball—that's a pretty neat trick. I've done it a few times, but it's not something you can do consistently. And it gets harder the older you get.

THIS ONE NEEDS a little explanation. This Booneism came from my Mesa days. At Mesa, I was the moneymaker. I found myself in the role of throwing the long pass and having to catch it, too. We had good people, but I was the one that had to make the big plays.

In 1993 my closest friend, Jerry Walsh, brought Mike Holder, OSU's legendary golf coach, out to hunt quail at my Mesa Vista Ranch. When I lost Jerry Walsh in 1995, Mike replaced him as my OSU best friend. A few years later, Mike brought the athletic director, Terry Don Phillips, out to the ranch. The conversation quickly turned to money. Over breakfast, I told Mike and Terry Don that I knew the $20 million they were asking from me to help renovate the football stadium was just the beginning.

"The stadium needs to be done, but that's not going to happen overnight," I said. "Even if we had all the money today, it would take us three years to accomplish anything, and that's not going to help recruiting now. There have to be things we can do immediately to improve our football program."

I knew they were having a tough time making ends meet while attempting to be competitive. I really started to get into it. How about the team's training table? Was the food good and healthy? I'd never had a good meal in Stillwater in my life. How about housing for the athletes? Was that up to par? Could they fit in their beds? Current players bring future recruits. You want these athletes to go home to Houston or Dallas or Tulsa or Oklahoma City for the summer and say, "Hey, you ought to see my school. There's some exciting stuff going on at OSU."

But Terry Don Phillips was hung up on the stadium. He wasn't kidding about needing the stadium. He thought once the stadium was taken care of, everything else would fall into place. Later Mike Holder said that when he and Terry Don were hunting together, he said, "Terry Don, Boone just served up the greatest gopher ball I've ever seen. Why didn't you just step up and knock it out of the park? You should have gone for some of his ideas and gone for the stadium later."

"Well, I just didn't want to get him distracted," Terry Don said. "I know we need that stadium."

In March 2002, I committed $70 million to OSU. At the time it was the largest donation to a university in Oklahoma, and it was for both sports and academics. In September 2003, it was announced during halftime of the Oklahoma State–Wyoming game that the stadium had been renamed Boone Pickens Stadium. Now I had real skin in the game. I certainly wasn't going to have my name on a loser. My giving to OSU had just begun.

It wasn't long before Mike Holder came out to see me at the ranch. "Boone, you keep talking about wanting to upgrade OSU. If you really want to get competitive, it's going to take $400 million."

I thought he was crazy, and I told him so.

"Then we won't be competitive," Mike said.

He knew that wasn't going to sit well with me. Like all great fund-raisers, Mike didn't have any problem asking for money. I'm always ready to give to a good cause, but I want to be convinced that the person who asks me is as committed to what we are going to do as I am. I wanted Mike to step up to the plate and show me his commitment to OSU just as he was asking me to do. It's absolutely essential to have somebody you trust manage your investment, especially when you're investing hundreds of millions of dollars.

The school's athletic director, Harry Birdwell, had announced his resignation in June 2005. I thought Mike was perfect for the AD job.

"If I give the money, what are you going to do, Mike?"

"Continue as golf coach," he said.

"Then put the plan back in the drawer."

Mike had been an All-American on the OSU golf team and later a winning golf coach. Mike had raised more than $10 million for his golf program. He had won eight national titles in thirty-two years and built the finest college golf course in the nation. The Cowboy golf program was the premier program in the NCAA, and this was one of our models for the other sports at OSU. The other model was our championship wrestling program, which had been winning national titles since the 1930s. Our two best coaches were Mike Holder and John Smith. They ran honest programs and won for the right reasons, and these were the two you wanted to clone. If both these guys had decided to coach football, you would have had two Vince Lombardis.

Mike is a fierce competitor and a family man, and I told him he would make a great athletic director. He said he'd think about it.

"I can tell you right now that I'm not going to donate the money unless you become athletic director," I told him. "Here's my take on you, Mike. You win a golf championship every four years. You've figured out a way to win at that game, and now you're going through life with your feet on the handlebars. You've never been tested at the level I'd like to test you. It's time for you to step up and take on a big challenge."

"What do you mean, feet on the handlebars?"

"You're a leader, and you need to lead at a higher level. That's what I mean."

Two weeks passed before he told me that he and Robbie had talked it over, and he would take the job as OSU's new AD. Just after Christmas, I called Mike and asked him to meet me in my office on December 29. He brought along Burns Hargis, the president of the OSU board of regents.

The night before, I'd tossed and turned and woke up Madeleine. "You're thinking about where you're going to get the money, aren't you?" she asked.

"Yeah. I sure am."

On the day we all met in my office, Mike showed me the spreadsheet he had prepared indicating how much it would take to build the stadium.

"Now how much is it that you're asking me to give?" I asked.

"I think the minimum is $165 million."

"OK," I said.

And that was that. Burns couldn't believe it. He thought I was bullshitting them. Holder knew I was serious.

Although it's pretty difficult to keep something that big that quiet, OSU didn't announce my donation immediately. On January 10, 2006, I flew to Stillwater for a press conference.

The following account appeared in OSU's *Daily O'Collegian* on January 11, 2006:

> When billionaire Boone Pickens gave his alma mater $70 million to renovate an aging football stadium in March 2003, it was a gift OSU had never seen before. When Pickens gave the university $165 million Tuesday morning, it was a gift like the nation had never seen before. According to university officials, Pickens' donation to OSU's athletic department is the single largest . . . to an

institute of higher learning in U.S. history—surpassing
Ralph Engelstad's 1998 donation to the University of North
Dakota by over $60 million.

The donation will be used to complete the west end
zone of the stadium that now bears Pickens' name, but the
Cowboy football program is not the only thing that will
benefit from the record-breaking contribution. OSU's soccer, track, equestrian, tennis and baseball teams are also
expected to receive facility upgrades during the next five
to 10 years. . . .

We all knew the $165 million was just a start on what would
eventually become a twenty-year master plan with an estimated
cost exceeding $700 million. The plan includes not only the sta-
dium but also an indoor practice facility for football, baseball, track,
and other sports, as well as upgraded facilities for track, tennis, and
soccer. There will also be a new equestrian center, a new baseball
stadium, and new outdoor practice fields.

Our plan was to invest the money and grow it by at least 20 percent annually. This was a tough order, but we had a lot of confidence at that point. Mike had already invested the golf team's
money with BP Capital, with extremely impressive results. "I may
not be the smartest person around, but when you've invested $6
million with someone and they turned it into $31 million, you feel
confident," he'd later say.

On December 29, the $165 million was wired to OSU. Twenty-
four hours later, the $165 million plus another $37 million from
Mike Holder's golf foundation was wired from OSU to BP Capital,
where it was invested in our fund. Fees charged by our fund are on
a 2-and-20 basis: 2 percent off the top and 20 percent on profits.

We waived all fees on the OSU investment. We have waived total fees of more than $60 million. All of the money is OSU's. At year end 2007, the $165 million had grown to $330 million.

This is far from just a case of wanting to have my name memorialized on a stadium. As I said on *HBO Real Sports,* "Hey, if somebody tops my gift, they can have their name on the stadium. I'll move over to the baseball field." And I meant it.

At one game, I was interviewed on the sideline by ESPN, and the broadcaster asked me when I'd last talked to head coach Mike Gundy. I told him that it had been the week before.

"What did you say to him?" the broadcaster asked.

"Play harder."

A year after my donation, I found another way to help OSU.

I went for my annual physical in 2006, and after my internist Gene Frenkel saw my physical, he said, "You're in good enough shape to be insured at standard rate." I had an immediate thought: *Can you monetize good health?* I discussed it with Bobby Stillwell, and we came up with a plan to help OSU through an innovative life-insurance program. Bobby brought Glenn Turner and John Ridings Lee in as consultants to help develop the plan. We brought Mike Holder in and told him to find OSU alums aged sixty-five to eighty-five who were insurable. The plan was to have the athletic foundation pay the premiums for ten-million-dollar policies on each individual, with the athletic department as the beneficiary. We were flying a little blind, but we soon found twenty-eight individuals, including myself, who qualified for the program.

It was the first time collegiate athletics had used a life-insurance program on such a grand scale. We called it Gift of a Lifetime, and it may be the first and last time a deal like this happens. Economic conditions have changed dramatically and made this program challenging to insurance companies. Mike Holder and Larry Reece were able to work in a very narrow window. While other schools were looking at it, OSU did it. Hats off to Mike and Larry for a job well done. Gift of a Lifetime will eventually net over $200 million for OSU. Leadership is everything.

When the twenty-eight people involved, including six couples, came to a September 2007 unveiling of the bronze plaque inscribed with their names, I got up and said, "This is monumental for the development of our university. We're in a deal together now. We're partners for life. The Gift of a Lifetime is one of our payoffs for staying healthy. I know you love our university. By staying healthy, you're giving a major gift to OSU."

You can't believe how many tears flowed. In my case, too. I choked up. I love tears at this kind of event. All of the participants there never dreamed that they would be able to give $10 million to the university they love so much. And the university has responded in kind by dedicating the opening game each football season to those who so generously participated in the first Gift of a Lifetime. All twenty-eight of us will sit together during that game and no doubt be recognized for this $200 million contribution.

At that point, my major concern was whether or not OSU alums would expect me to carry the ball by myself or whether they would start to pitch in and support their alma mater. The response has been overwhelming. I've met some tremendous people, and they all want the same thing I do: help OSU excel.

I'm eighty years old. I want results now. I've been impatient throughout my career, and I want to see progress. That doesn't mean winning every game, but then again, why not? In the past, OSU was a stepping stone to somewhere else for coaches. Part of it was our fault; the athletic department didn't have the budget to pay coaches and assistants competitive salaries. They wanted to come through and move up. No longer. We're now paying our coaching staff at the top level.

Victory—that's what it's about. But victory through playing by the rules and doing things the right way. I've said repeatedly that if the program ever becomes dishonest, its most enthusiastic supporter will be a goner. My gifts will live on, but I'll be gone. Currently there's no end to the help that I'll give my university.

We are on a tremendous roll at OSU and continue to improve leadership at the school. We just landed our best recruit since Barry Sanders when Burns Hargis agreed to accept the presidency of OSU. He is one of the most respected business leaders in Oklahoma and understands both business and government. As the former chairman of OSU's board of regents and the former president of the Bank of Oklahoma, Burns has a keen vision for the future of OSU. He will make it a great institution. He knows he has my total support.

I like to think I'm as creative in my philanthropy as I am in my business. Another example of this is my gift of $100 million to the University of Texas System, split between UT Southwestern Medical Center in Dallas and the M.D. Anderson Cancer Center in Houston with the stipulation that both institutions invest the money and grow it into $1 billion ($500 million each) within twenty-five years. If they fail, they must give whatever they've made to OSU. That won't happen. The University of Texas is never going to write a check to Oklahoma State for anything. I hope I'm around to see how this plays out. Competition in giving is as important as competition in sports or business. A rising tide lifts all boats. The University of Texas will deliver on its $1 billion contract, and that will be 10-for-1 on every dollar I gave.

Giving involves more than money; it also involves time, and I've worked with my wife, Madeleine, on some interesting projects. Our relationship began in February 2005. I called Madeleine and invited her to the ranch, where I was spending the weekend with a group of friends.

"Are you a gambler?" I asked her, in the hope that she would be willing to take a chance. "I'm not a gambler, but I am curious," she said when she accepted the invitation. I flew her out—or at least tried to fly her from her home in Southern California to the ranch. First, I sent a Citation 10. When it arrived it had a mechanical problem. So NetJets said, "Hang on and we'll send a Falcon 2000," which got to Carlsbad and also had mechanical problems. NetJets' malfunctions were now stacking up at the airport. Finally, they sent a Gulfstream 4, which Madeleine knew wouldn't break down. She was the widow of the late Allen E. Paulson, the founder of Gulfstream.

Madeleine is a devoted animal lover, everything from dogs to horses. She's owned many legendary Thoroughbreds, including Cigar, who won the Breeders' Cup Classic and equaled Citation's all-time record winning streak of sixteen races in a row. She was born into a life of adventure. Her father, a British Army officer, met her Lebanese mother in Cairo during World War II. He was in the British 8th Army under General Montgomery and was dispatched to Libya. He was so taken with the woman he'd left behind that he told his commanding officer, "I've got to go back and marry her."

The officer said, "I can give you the time off, but I can't get you there." So her father hitchhiked through war zones in Libya and Egypt to return to Cairo and marry Madeleine's mother. When Madeleine and her twin sister, Christine, turned eighteen, they were living in England. Their mother gave them each 100 pounds sterling and a one-way ticket to anywhere they wanted to live in the world. They chose the Bahamas, since it was a British colony and they were British citizens. Two weeks after they moved there, they got a call from their mother. She was in a sanitarium with tuberculosis, and they realized that in sending them away she had saved them from incarceration: in those days, children of those infected with TB were sent away with the patient. What a selfless gift she gave her daughters.

I never intended to marry again. But Madeleine is extraordinary. She's high energy, positive, passionate about many causes, and pretty easy to look at. I find her endlessly captivating. And at my age, a love affair has to move along pretty quickly.

After I asked her to marry me, we went to New York to pick out a ring. She picked a nice, but simple, diamond heart ring. Being competitive in everything I do, I didn't want to buy her that ring only to discover later that she owned a bigger ring. I pulled her aside and told her, "Madeleine, I don't want to be out-ringed." She thought it was charming—and very Texan. We were married in Del Mar, California, in July 2005.

Less than a month later, Hurricane Katrina slammed into New Orleans. Night after night, we watched the devastation on television, wincing over the relief effort. Rescuers were putting people in helicopters but forcing them to leave their pets. We watched one man who'd been on his roof for a couple of days. His family had been rescued, but he'd insisted on staying behind with his dog. Finally the man became too sick to stay; rescuers flew in by helicopter and forced him to leave. Tragically, they made him leave his dog behind. We could see the dog looking up with a desperate look. *Why are you leaving me?*

Madeleine started to cry.

"What would you do," she asked me, "if they said you could leave but you'd have to abandon your dog?" She was talking about my papillon, Murdock.

"I'd tell them to pitch me an inner tube, and I'd take my chances with Murdock."

Madeleine spent the next several hours working the phone. When she came back, she had a plan. "I've got to get to Baton Rouge," she said.

"OK, I'm coming with you."

She had called the Federal Emergency Management Agency (FEMA) and the military. Both were too busy with people to help with pets. Madeleine enlisted the local humane society and leased a Continental Airlines 737. Operation Orphans of the Storm was born. She sent our ranch manager out to gather supplies and pet food at the ranch and in nearby Pampa. We cleaned everybody out.

I flew with Madeleine and five of our people from the ranch in our G4 to Baton Rouge. We'd arranged to have two hundred abandoned pets waiting for us to load onto the chartered 737. But in the chaos of the hurricane and the slow relief effort, there were only forty dogs on the ground when we got there. We had room for two hundred dogs on the plane. My wife said, "Help!" We needed to find another one hundred sixty dogs and cats.

Hilton Cole of the Baton Rouge Animal Control Center had an old truck with a gooseneck trailer. Hilton, our ranch manager, Keith Boone, and I drove to Louisiana State University, where homeless dogs and other pets were being sheltered. It was chaos. Thousand of dogs. Stressed-out workers. We loaded about one hundred forty animals into the trailer and made our way back to the airport.

The pets were taken onboard, then flown to shelters in the San

Francisco area, San Diego, and Denver, where residents could con-
tribute to the Katrina recovery effort simply by adopting a dog or
a cat. All the pets' photographs were posted on petfinders.com.

Remember the dog on the roof that first stunned Madeleine into
action? That dog was on our airlift. The dog not only survived but,
through the work of volunteers, he was reunited with his master.
That relief effort, which included two more 737 trips from Baton
Rouge to the West Coast, lasted a few weeks.

In many cases, you don't have to go to creative lengths in your
giving. You just have to stand up for what you believe is right—and
fight what you know is wrong. This is what happened to Madeleine
and me in the summer of 2006.

We were in Corpus Christi, being honored by the local SPCA for
our work in airlifting the dogs and cats of Hurricane Katrina, when
a woman came up to Madeleine at the luncheon and said, "There's
a really serious issue I have to talk to you about." Then she said
the two words that even a longtime, dedicated horsewoman like
Madeleine hadn't heard before: "Horse slaughter."

Madeleine would eventually learn the whole shameful and
shocking story. Horses were systematically being slaughtered for
meat. Although the slaughter of horses for human consumption is
illegal in the United States, foreign-owned companies were using
federal loopholes to kill horses in the United States and ship the
horse meat to foreign countries. A movement to stop the slaughter
had been underway since 2003, when news broke that Ferdinand,
the 1986 Kentucky Derby winner, had ended up in a Japanese
slaughterhouse. The American Horse Slaughter Prevention Act, a
bipartisan bill to end horse slaughter, was being supported by tens
of thousands of people across the country, but the organization
needed help in Texas. Two of the three foreign-owned slaughter-

houses were located there, and although polls showed that 70 percent of the public was against horse slaughter, powerful farm and
ranch groups—and their lobbyists—had kept the bill off the floor
of Congress. The defenders of horse slaughter were forceful. They
argued that the people who were against it were tree huggers and
pet nuts who would regulate even "fish in the aquarium."

Madeleine was outraged, and after she told me about it I was
outraged, too. We joined the fight, and it quickly turned into a cru-
sade. Letters and e-mails, passionately for and against horse slaughter, poured into our offices. The media exposure exploded. In the
summer of 2006, I was talking horses almost as much as oil and gas.
Finally, Madeleine and I went to Washington, where on July 25,
2006, I testified before Congress in support of the American Horse
Slaughter Prevention Act.

"Texas has a dirty little secret that should shame all of us who
live here," I said, calling to shut down the slaughterhouses. Near
the end of the proceedings, Representative Joe Barton asked me
whether we could reach a compromise.

"I don't know, Mr. Chairman," I said. "How do you compromise
slaughter?"

While the battle to end horse slaughter had taken place in
Congress, in the end it was a judicial ruling that closed the slaugh-
ter plants in Texas. The United States Court of Appeals for the Fifth
Circuit upheld a Texas ban on the practice. But the fight is not over.
Efforts are underway in Washington to allow a return to slaughter.

So, says Madeleine, "We have to start all over again." I ride for the
brand, and Madeleine's the brand. Whatever happens next, I'll be
there by her side.

CHAPTER 10

"Roll Up the Maps!"

Booneism #23: If you're on the right side of the issue, just keep driving until you hear glass breaking. Don't quit.

ONE ADVANTAGE OF staying active as you get older is that projects you've spent a long time fighting for—and even projects that have failed—can finally see success.

September 19, 2007: Times Square, New York

The logo of Clean Energy Fuels swirled on the multicolored, computerized, circular billboard outside of NASDAQ's headquarters in Times Square. NASDAQ WELCOMES CLEAN ENERGY FUELS CORP, the billboard proclaimed. Inside the exchange, I joined with Andrew Littlefair and we both rang the bell to start trading that day. This traditional ceremony recognized Clean Energy's arrival as a public company.

Clean Energy Fuels was the eighth company I'd taken public and my first on the NASDAQ. It was a stirring climax to a decade's worth of hard work and perseverance. The foundation of the company lies

in a long-held belief that natural gas—clean, cheap, and domestic—
is a superior fuel and should be moved into transportation to reduce
our escalating dependence on foreign oil and address our ever-
suffocating pollution from vehicle emissions.

After NASDAQ's opening bell from nine-thirty to noon, Andrew
and I did interviews with CNBC, Dow Jones Newswires, *The Wall
Street Journal,* and *Barron's* about the potential of natural gas and
Clean Energy Fuels. The stock rose $3 that day, which I believe hap-
pened because natural gas as a superior alternative fuel is largely
an untold story. It's an example of the power of recognizing a good
idea, investing in it, and then sticking with it through thick and thin.

Good ideas never die. Not if you have the ability—and the
longevity—to ride them out. Clean Energy is an ideal example of
this. It's all about recognizing something that most people didn't
and many still don't. It's also about timing. I was early in my bet on
natural gas but not wrong.

> **Booneism #24:** *If you're going to run with the big dogs,*
> *you have to get out from under the porch.*

THE IDEA THAT eventually became Clean Energy began in 1988.

I thought I could make it work in three years. I was off by almost
twenty. I don't know that I've ever been this far ahead of the curve.
I'd bet Mesa on the price of natural gas, and I'd lost because of my
timing. That doesn't change the fact that natural gas is still the superior fuel: 30 percent cheaper and producing at least 75 percent
fewer smog-forming chemicals than gasoline and 83 percent fewer
than diesel. It is also environmentally superior and without the
threat of oil spills and other hazards. Best of all, it's domestic, which
frees it from foreign pricing and foreign influence.

In a speech I gave years ago, someone questioned the safety of putting natural gas in cars.

"Let me ask you, do you cook with natural gas on your stove?" I said.

"Yes, of course."

"OK, let's do an experiment. Let's put natural gas in your car and gasoline in your stove."

"Gasoline in my house!" they exclaimed. "Are you crazy?"

That's the point. The idea that gasoline is safer than natural gas is just wrong.

In late 1988 I pressed Mesa's bet that gas prices would rise. Tenneco was auctioning off their Mid Continent Division, which was primarily its Hugoton gas field reserves in southwest Kansas, where we already had a sizable stake. It was a natural fit with Mesa. We paid $715 million and acquired the reserves, giving Mesa 1.6 trillion cubic feet of natural gas in the Hugoton field.

"We're OK as long as natural gas doesn't go below $2.32," I said at the time. Then natural gas began sliding, first a tremor, then an avalanche. It went down to $2, then $1.80, then $1.50. Then it dropped to under $1.

It quickly became evident that I'd made a king-sized mistake. I began making some comparisons. If you take natural gas, which works as a fuel just as well as gasoline, and get it in the transportation fuel market, then you wouldn't compare its price to that of oil. You would compare it to gasoline.

One Mcf of natural gas is equal to eight gallons of gasoline. So if gasoline is selling for $1.50 a gallon, as it was back then, you would multiply the price by eight, which would give you $12 Mcf for the natural gas. It would be a huge increase over the $1 Mcf that natural gas was selling for. If natural gas sold at parity with gasoline, it would be cost neutral to the consumer and a huge increase for a domestic natural resource, translating into profits, taxes, and a reduction in foreign oil: a ten-strike.

Of course, there are some production costs involved. You have to compress it, and you have to transport it. Even after those costs, we would have an enormous upgrade in price if we could get it in competition with gasoline and diesel. Yes, a little dreamy, but my back was against the wall once again.

I looked at the numbers and I thought, *How do I get from A to B?*

I believed that I could just stick with three points—clean, cheap, and domestic—and sell the idea. But it wasn't as easy as I thought in 1988. Nobody was concerned about foreign oil imports back then. If it was really cheap, they'd talk to you. If it wasn't, they weren't interested in the other two points. Natural gas wasn't being used much as a vehicular fuel in the United States at that time even though it had long been a fuel staple in foreign countries such as Argentina. The United States Postal Service has been using alternative fuels since the 1970s and compressed natural-gas-powered vehicles since 1993. An even earlier natural gas innovator, Disneyland in California, had been using natural gas to propel its Jungle Cruise boats since the 1970s. By the late 1980s, many claimed that our dream of using natural gas in other vehicles was pure Fantasyland.

Still, it wasn't an impossible task. There are more than 250 million vehicles in the United States. My goal was to get 1 million of them on natural gas. However, it soon became clear that our target wasn't consumer automobiles but fleet operators. All we needed to make our business work was 100,000 vehicles, not 1 million.

It doesn't take long to reach a critical mass of fleet vehicles that justifies building a fueling station. For example, twenty transit buses, the equivalent of six hundred cars, would be enough to make it feasible to build one fueling station. Our goal was to get into the fuel supply business: building, owning, and operating natural gas fueling stations for commercial fleets. I also figured that fleet adoption would lead to the creation of a large national infrastructure for natural-gas-powered vehicles, which in turn would support a broader market.

To get started in the early 1990s, we met with the American Gas Association, which represents two hundred local utility companies that deliver natural gas to millions of homes, businesses, and industries throughout the United States. Natural gas was already being used in some commercial vehicle fleets, and there was a fledgling movement to expand such usage. It was being led by such companies as Southern California Gas, Equitable Gas in Pittsburgh, and Brooklyn Union in New York.

I took over the leadership of this movement and became chairman of the Natural Gas Vehicle Coalition, a national trade organization of one hundred or so utility companies dedicated to the development of a growing, sustainable, and profitable market for vehicles powered by natural gas. From Washington, D.C., to Los Angeles, I stumped for natural gas as a transportation fuel. In the press, my colleagues at the Natural Gas Vehicle Coalition predicted that by 2000 there would be 5.5 million natural-gas-powered cars and trucks on American roads. They offered this prediction at a time when there were at most thirty thousand natural gas vehicles in the country. A huge miss.

All of this made sense at the time. "In Mexico City, vehicles are shut down every other day if they burn gasoline. That could happen in Los Angeles. Natural gas is going to be the cheap way out. We should stop building up the infrastructure of the Middle East and start building it in the United States," I added, referring to our dependence on foreign oil. "It's going to happen. The question is, how fast?" When I said that natural gas prices could double by 1995 thanks to its increased use in vehicles, there didn't seem to be a believer in the crowd. For damned good reason.

I was wrong.

Not long ago, I was speaking in Midland before several thousand people. Jay Rosser was sitting in the front row, and he couldn't hear any of my answers. Nobody could. Five minutes passed before Jay finally interrupted the event and said, "Boone, I don't think people can hear you. Where's your microphone?"

I reached up to my lapel. Sure enough, no microphone. Finally, after fiddling around, I found it. I was sitting on it. After putting the microphone back where it was supposed to be, I told the audience, "You can tell them that the first ten minutes he talked out of his ass." That comment drew so many laughs that it ended up running in the *Midland Reporter-Telegram* the next day.

The natural gas vehicle business was catching on in some markets. In April 1993, President Bill Clinton signed an executive order directing federal agencies to increase purchases of alternative-fuel vehicles by 50 percent; the government target was to buy 35,000 vehicles a year by 1997. Clinton named Texas land commissioner Garry Mauro, a champion of natural gas vehicles, to chair a federal task force that would advise Energy Secretary Hazel O'Leary on the fleet conversion. I suggested publicly that the president double his alternative fleet order to 100,000 vehicles and use natural gas to power them. "That alone would send a clear message to the Big Three and the public." I meant the Big Three U.S. automakers, which have been slow to embrace alternative fuels programs. Not long after this, President Clinton appointed me to his Natural Gas Task Force.

By then we had formed Mesa Environmental to promote natural gas as a transportation fuel. It was really an equipment company. We began by focusing on producing under-the-hood components to convert vehicles to run on natural gas instead of gasoline. We set up an office in Fort Worth and bought an under-the-hood engine technology company that provided our Mesa GEM (gas engine management) Kit, a conversion kit to enable vehicles to run on natural gas. We were one of the first three under-the-hood kit manufacturers on the market. GM and Ford were already using under-the-hood kits in a limited way.

I was working morning, noon, and night. We were trying to take the lead in every aspect of the business, while the people who were in the business were all trying to sell out to us. That should have been the tip-off. I'd had a good idea but no experience in manufacturing anything. Our under-the-hood conversion equipment was inferior.

Most major automakers gave lip service to alternative-fuel vehicles. They could have produced mass-market natural gas vehicles if they'd wanted to. But they didn't want to. With few exceptions, bureaucracies do not embrace change readily. Change also didn't come easily to industry leaders like Enron's Ken Lay. Ken and I had heated exchanges over my conviction that America should be redirecting natural gas away from power generation and into transportation. I felt that other fuels—nuclear and clean coal, to name two—could serve power generation much better. Ken, however, was a strong advocate of natural gas in power generation at the lowest possible price because Enron was a large power producer, not a natural gas producer.

We quickly won a couple of big contracts for our under-the-hood conversion kits. One was with UPS to convert one thousand of their vehicles. Another was with the United States Postal Service to convert three thousand. I was reelected to a second term as chairman of the Natural Gas Vehicle Coalition.

Next we began pitching to different cities around the country. The goal was to get them to switch their fleets—primarily trash and transit trucks—from gasoline and diesel to natural gas. The advantages were clear: putting one trash truck on natural gas was the equivalent of taking 325 cars off the road. I'll say it again: natural gas is a great fuel. Municipalities began to take notice because it made sense. Today, of the nearly 2,500 buses in the Los Angeles Transit Authority fleet, 2,250 are fueled by natural gas. That number is second only to the fleet of natural gas buses in Beijing, which numbers 4,000.

Our CEO, Andrew Littlefair, identified prospective cities. Andrew and I work closely together. He was an aide to President Ronald Reagan from 1983 to 1987 and then came to Mesa as my executive assistant. Andrew was given responsibility at Mesa for our natural-gas-vehicle fueling, as well as our state and federal lobbying. Kind of an unusual combination, but that sometimes happened at Mesa: you ended up with a potpourri of assignments.

Phoenix seemed like the perfect place to start our campaign to get cities to convert their fleets to natural gas. Phoenix owned thousands of municipal vehicles. Andrew was our advance man. Typically, we'd have Andrew meet a prospective city's mayor, or maybe a local congressman, or even the state's governor, and set up a dinner the night before our presentation. We'd have a press conference the next day, where we'd make a proposal to convert their city's vehicle fleets to natural gas as long as the city bought its natural gas from us. Once the proposal was accepted, we'd put natural gas fueling stations in convenient locations.

In May 1992, Mesa offered to convert the entire vehicle fleet of the state of Arizona from gasoline and diesel to natural gas. It would be seven years before the state would even consider our proposal. We made the same offer to the state of Louisiana. We still haven't heard back from them.

Our road show to sell natural gas to municipal fleets was pretty good theater. The problem was that we never pulled it off quite as we planned. Our instincts about natural gas as a transportation fuel were correct, but it was way too early for it to happen. Again, I had a timing problem, not a vision problem. None of the cities or states we pitched bought into our proposal. So we took another route.

In 1994, we approached SuperShuttle with the idea of converting their vans to run on compressed natural gas. The company's blue vans transport travelers door-to-door from homes and hotels to and from airports. Back in the mid-1990s, the vans were fueled by propane; we thought SuperShuttle could be a high-profile platform for natural gas fuel. Unfortunately, at the time we didn't know the depth of SuperShuttle's problems. SuperShuttle was in dire straits: no profits, no credit lines, no new equipment. They had vans working at seven or eight airports, but some of the vehicles had 1 million miles on them.

Andrew and I went to the City of Opportunity—Gardena, California, just south of Los Angeles—to meet with the company's founder, Mitchell Rouse, at his taxicab office. Mitch operates more taxis than anyone in America. Back then, he was operating 1,000 cabs in Southern California in addition to SuperShuttle, which had 230 vans in Los Angeles and 400 more in Phoenix, San Francisco, Dallas, and Miami.

Mitch wore a poker face. Later he'd admit that his company was in such bad shape that he'd have accepted an offer to run his vans on carrot juice if the supplier had offered to help him out of his financial pinch. His company was being strangled by workers' compensation costs. If he didn't get a cash infusion fast, he was going to lose his shuttle business.

When Andrew and I walked in, it was like the Red Cross arriving in a war zone. The deal we offered Mitch was to finance a new natural-gas-powered fleet for SuperShuttle. All they had to do was agree to buy their natural gas from us. Mitch stood up and extended his hand, and we shook on the deal. We were both desperate.

When we looked at the company's financial statements, it became clear that financing the fleet would just be a Band-Aid on SuperShuttle's deeper problems. Our investment eventually exceeded $7 million: $5 million for the new compressed-natural-gas-powered fleet of 200 vans and $2.1 million in working capital. We also built three natural gas fueling stations so the company could buy their fuel from us. It was now obvious that we were hell-bent on making this idea work. We were now committed.

It turned out to be a good investment. Today SuperShuttle has close to 1,200 vans, and a significant portion of them run on natural gas. The money we loaned the company to buy their vans and to return to solid financial footing would come back to us at a critical period a few years later, especially when the $2.1-million note that we'd assumed when we'd bought the fueling business from Mesa came due.

By 1995, the price of natural gas was falling. With our debt rising and our stock price dropping, Mesa's problems were just too deep. I believed in the natural gas fueling business, but it wasn't going to happen fast enough to bail out Mesa.

In 1996, after Richard Rainwater's equity infusion led to his takeover at Mesa, I attempted to explain the potential of our natural gas fueling company to him and his associates. They not only didn't understand it but they also had no interest in what I had to say about anything. On at least two more occasions, I sat down with Rainwater and Hersh and told them that the company's natural gas fueling business had a real opportunity to grow. They just weren't interested. Less than a year later, when they had done nothing with the fueling business, I told Andrew, "Let's buy it."

They accepted our $1.1-million offer, which included three fueling stations, a repair truck, some tools, and—we were convinced— unlimited potential. Of course, the business also came with the $2.1 million receivable from SuperShuttle.

Since we got a note for $2.1 million and paid only $1.1 million for the fueling business, you're probably thinking, *Boone got it for nothing, and they gave him a tip.* Not exactly. I took a chance on the $2.1-million note. However, I did know Mitch, and I thought he was good for it.

Shortly after we bought the fueling business, we moved it to Southern California and made Andrew CEO. Andrew moved his wife and kids into a rented house in Newport Beach and launched our fueling business. Great businesses start in unlikely places. This was the case of the company that became Clean Energy. To say that this start-up was done on a shoestring budget is a stretch. Andrew used his local Mail Boxes Etc. to send and receive faxes. He sent his letters to our Dallas office to be typed and mailed. He worked off his kitchen table until we could rent a small two-room office.

We had cultivated relationships with Southern California Gas, including its chairman, Warren Mitchell, who had succeeded me as chairman of the Natural Gas Vehicle Coalition in 1994. By 1996, the Southern California Gas Company had thirty-three natural gas fueling stations, but the Public Utility Commission decided against allowing the utilities to spend any more ratepayer money on natural gas fueling. The commission wanted the public utilities out of the business within five years. Warren felt his stations needed to be sold to someone who would grow the business. Andrew and I had dinner with Warren and his assistant at the Crescent Club in Dallas to discuss our buying SoCal's stations.

"We can't put any equity into it," I told Warren.

"Well, you don't need to. We'll just take debt on the thing. We need to get rid of these stations," he responded.

After dinner, we walked outside, out of earshot of Andrew, and I asked Warren to tell it to me straight. "Do you think this thing could ever be a business?"

"Boone, I've been a good friend of yours for a long time. If I were you, I wouldn't do it. I don't think this business is going to make it."

"What will we do with Andrew?" I asked. "He'll be out of a job."

"I don't know what will happen to Andrew, but I just don't think this will work. It's a pretty iffy market, and it's going to take considerable time to get this business off the ground." He wasn't kidding. We often remind Warren, who is now chairman of Clean Energy Fuels, that he didn't want us to even get in the business.

We bought all the stations from SoCal in June 1997. Again, a lucky break. The purchase price was $3.6 million, but we didn't put up any cash. We paid it out quarterly over five years at 6 percent interest. Most importantly, we picked up a franchise in Southern California. We bought out the only player in the market with no money down.

Most of SoCal's stations were losers. These had been the company's first fueling stations, and the company hadn't understood our anchor-tenant model; they'd just put the stations in random locations in the middle of nowhere. Of the stations we bought from SoCal, only about ten were worth a damn.

We ended up closing fifteen of those original thirty-three. In the first year of operation, which really was only half of 1997, we sold the equivalent of 2 million gasoline gallons of natural gas fuel. The next year, we did 5 million gallons, and then the next year we did 7.5 million gallons. By 2000, I had fed about $3.5 million of my own money into the natural gas fueling business.

I was under pressure, and I felt that selling some of the fueling business was the best thing to do. You could have bought half of the business for $2 million in 2000. In June 2001, I sold 75 percent of it for $21 million to British Columbia Gas and Westport Innovations. That same year, we changed the name of the company to Clean Energy Fuels.

In December 2002, we acquired more natural gas fueling operations from Blue Energy, a spin-off of Public Service Company of Colorado, and TXU Corporation. We also got into the liquefied natural gas (LNG) business that year. We went to Vancouver to see John Reid, the CEO of BC Gas, now called Terasen. John is a very distinguished, British-born businessman. He asked me to speak to his board. I believed natural gas was headed up, way up. I suggested we take an aggressive position on natural gas futures. I told them we would make a lot of money and then we could sell the positions to pay for the overhead of the company, just as Ron Bassett and I had done at my desk in my last decade at Mesa. That scared the hell out of John Reid. He thought we were gunslingers in the futures markets. He just said, "Oh my God, Boone, we can't do that!" In 2004, we made that play and picked up $40 million for Clean Energy.

Perseus, a private equity firm, became a shareholder after our deal with Public Service Company of Colorado. By 2004, Perseus and I put some additional money into the company, and the

Canadians didn't. I got a little bit more ownership, whittling the Canadians' ownership down to about 43 percent. I had 22 percent and Perseus about 25 percent. Andrew and I continued to give presentations to persuade municipalities to convert their trash and transit fleets to natural gas. The more I spoke about the advantages of natural gas, the more I sold myself. I was absolutely convinced that we were sitting on the wave of the future and natural gas fueling was finally coming into its own. I decided I wanted to own a majority interest again. I had sold myself on my own deal. It was the classic "Roll Up the Maps" story.

In the 1950s, there was a rancher in Midland named Buck York. Buck had watched Hugh and Bill Liedtke, George H. W. Bush, and other guys come to Midland in the 1940s and get rich on oil deals. So he thinks, *Hell, I can do that. I just need to get me a geologist.* So he hires a geologist and tells him, "I'm watching all these other guys get rich. Get a good prospect, and we'll take it to Dallas and sell it. Draw up some maps and put a lot of color on them. Investors like color. That's what sells. Make two or three cross sections. They like those, too."

A couple of weeks later, the young geologist returns and says, "Mr. York, I've got the maps ready. Do you want to see them?"

And Buck York says, "No. They got a lot of color?"

"Yeah, they got a lot of color."

"OK, good. Let's go to Dallas."

The next day, they're in Dallas and Buck York's got the right people in the room. His geologist goes through the deal, which Buck has never seen until now. The investors

are really getting interested, and so is Buck. They're leaning over the table and starting to loosen their ties and col-
lars and asking all the right questions. Just as everything is
getting pretty serious, Buck asks for a break. "I need to
speak to my geologist."

The two of them go out in the hallway, where Buck tells
his geologist,"Roll up the maps and tell those son of bitches
this deal is sold!"

Buck had fallen in love with his own deal—and that's exactly
what I did. I did a Buck York. He would have been proud of me. I
fell in love with my own deal. I bought Clean Energy back.

By 2005, the year our funds would earn more than $1 billion,
our natural gas fueling business kept looking better. In 2001, I had
sold 75 percent of the fueling business for $21 million. In 2005,
I bought back 40 percent of what I'd sold to the Canadians for
$43 million. Now I own 60 percent of the company, a position that
is now worth around $400 million.

Thank you, Mr. and Mrs. Rainwater.

CLEAN ENERGY (NASDAQ: CLNE) went public on May 25, 2007.
The market cap of the company is $625 million.

Today, 8 million vehicles worldwide are running on natural gas.
When we started fifteen years ago, there were around 30,000 in the
United States. We fuel close to 15,000 vehicles daily at our 185 stations, and we're building 20 to 40 new stations each year. Today
almost 25 percent of all transit buses are running on natural gas,
with 25 percent growth annually. Of the 200,000 trash trucks now
running in the United States, only 1 percent are on natural gas. We
feel the natural-gas-fueled trash truck sector will also grow by 3 to

4 percent a year, which means between 6,000 and 8,000 trash trucks going to natural gas in 2009. Within a decade, we expect that half of America's trash truck fleet will be fueled by natural gas.

We've been in the business longer than any of our competitors. We are operating in eleven states, as well as Canada and Peru, and we have the most experienced team. We produce our own liquefied natural gas and haul it in our fleet of sixty LNG tanker trailers. We're also building a new liquefied natural gas plant, the first in California, which will open in 2008. California is the leader in environmental causes. I always feel that when California pushes, the rest of the United States responds at some point, because new things usually travel from west to east.

Our job now is to grow this business. I think we should be able to triple its size within a few years. We currently have $120 million targeted for expansion. We're based in Seal Beach with 7 sales offices in 6 states, 135 employees, and a sales staff of 40, including Jim Harger, our first hire at Pickens Fuel Corp., and one of the best salesmen I've ever seen. Harger told me the other day, "If it hadn't been for Boone Pickens, there would be no natural gas fueling business."

>   **Booneism #25:** *"Son, you've been invited to a duck din*
>   *ner. But you've got to bring the duck."*

I'D HEARD FOR years about how China's relentless economic growth is affecting global energy markets, and I wanted to see it firsthand. We'd also been encouraged by the Chinese to look at the potential of establishing natural gas fueling stations there. In the summer of 2007, we took our first and last trip to China, where energy demand is reaching crisis levels. My longtime friends

L.A. county supervisor Michael Antonovich and his beautiful wife, Christina, hosted our visit.

Our group included my wife, Madeleine, Andrew Littlefair, Jay Rosser, and Becky Quick, the CNBC *Squawk Box* anchor, who went along to film regular CNBC segments on the trip, which the network called "Boone's Excellent Adventure." We flew out of San Diego at 6 p.m.

Upon arriving in Beijing at ten the next night, we got off in the sweltering heat and horrendous pollution. The air quality is so poor that I later said that if they held the 2008 Beijing Summer Olympics on the night we got to China, the 100-meter dash would have to be a relay.

Even at night, the traffic congestion was so bad that the government was preparing to take 3 million cars off the roads as a test of ways to improve air quality for the Olympics. At our hotel, the thermostats were permanently fixed at 80 degrees as part of a country-wide energy conservation move. The escalators were set on sensors so as not to waste energy until someone stepped up to them. Not a bad idea.

The next morning we awoke to find a nation on the brink, proof of what happens when demand obliterates supply. China is a country of 1.3 billion people fighting for air, water, space, and fuel. We had ten days of back-to-back meetings, speeches, and government-sponsored dinners and events. I spoke to the American Chamber of Commerce and met with chief executives of the China Offshore Oil Corporation and officials from the China Power Petrochemical Corporation.

The sheer number of vehicles already powered by natural gas in China proved that there was a market: 81,257 light-duty vehicles, 36,996 buses, and 82,250 vehicles that serve a wide range of service sectors. We visited the Beijing Public Transit Authority, whose 4,000 buses run on natural gas. However, they're equipped with inefficient, antiquated engines. At our last meeting, at a power company, a group of executives told us that they had built thirty-three natural-gas-powered power plants along a pipeline on the assurance that the gas had been discovered to fuel the plants. It turned out that they hadn't discovered nearly as much natural gas as they thought they had.

"Can you get the natural gas for us?" one executive asked me. It was obvious that they had real problems. They had built plants and didn't have gas, and they wanted to know if we had gas. The only thing we could do was bring liquefied natural gas into the country.

They were inviting me to a duck dinner. Only I had to bring the duck.

"Go talk to the Russians or the Iranians. They've got the gas," I said. It was obvious that they had already tried that idea.

For us to bring natural gas into China, we'd have to arrange for liquefied natural gas to come by tanker, probably from the Middle East. This goes to show how fortunate we are in America, where natural gas is domestically produced and readily available.

China is a long way to go when you've got plenty of deals in your own backyard. It's interesting that today Clean Energy Fuels is now twice the size that Mesa was back when we left in 1996. Richard Rainwater got Mesa. I took the natural gas fueling business and the trading operation. It was one of the best deals I ever made. I never root for anyone to drill a dry hole, but I want to do better than they do. Not only is it my nature but it also helps to have someone against whom I can benchmark my performance. When I left Mesa in 1996, that person became Richard Rainwater. From 1997 to 2007, Rainwater and Pioneer, the company that eventually emerged from Mesa, earned a profit of about $900 million. They had a particularly tough go at first, losing $1.7 billion during their first three years. By comparison, when I started BP Capital, I had a desk, a telephone, and no debt. During that same period from 2000 to 2007, BP Capital made a total profit of $8 billion. Best of all, unlike Pioneer, we carried no debt.

CHAPTER 11

Mixing Oil and Water

Booneism #26: When you're hunting elephants, don't get distracted chasing rabbits.

Y*OU'RE NEVER DONE until you're done.*

That's the only way to approach life and business. People frequently ask me why I get involved in a big project when I won't ever see the results. Well, if I'm not here when the project is finished, I'll at least be here when it's a long way down the track. This mentality keeps you active, in the game. *I'm not sure that it doesn't keep you alive.*

I've always been in a hurry. I know I'm racing against time. You have to keep going after things, whether it's deals or football games or repetitions on a weight machine. I compete against everybody, including myself. I'm never *against* anybody. I just compete against them. People say that when you get older, you get conservative, complacent, and tired. In my view, you can or you can't. That's up to you. However, the last quarter of a lifetime, like the last minutes of a game, is the stretch where one is tested the most. Once you slow down, it's hard to start up again. When I wake up every morning, I know what I'm going to do. I've said many times, I've seen guys who can't get forty hours out of a week, and I've seen guys who can get forty hours out of a day. But I start the day at six in the morning, and my trainer shows up at six-thirty. I typically work out for forty-five minutes and get into the office before the market opens. I've already talked to the traders at least three times before I show up at BP Capital at eight.

At eighty, am I excited to wake up? Sure I am. That mentality keeps you young, active, and engaged. Or at least I think it does, and that's good enough. Thinking you're too old to do something only accelerates old age, feeds the feeling of fallibility, and leads to idleness. But don't be unrealistic. I know I can't broad jump twenty feet any more.

Engagement. Involvement. Constant action. That's the way to live your life. Wake up every morning believing you're going to live forever. No limits. No restrictions. Our water and wind deals are the epitome of this mentality. I may not be here at their fruition, but I'll know how they're going to turn out long before I'm gone.

As with oil, water is finite and subject to increasing demand. Studies and reports estimate that 75 percent of the planet is water, yet less than 1 percent is drinkable. According to a United Nations report, 1.2 billion people around the world don't have access to safe water. Within twenty-five years, the United Nations Environment Programme calculated, "half the world's population could have trouble finding enough freshwater for drinking and irrigation." The United Nations report also calculated that "almost 2 million children die each year for want of a glass of clean water and adequate sanitation" and that by 2050, 7 billion people in sixty countries could face water scarcity issues.

"Of all the social and natural crises we humans face, the water crisis is the one that lies at the heart of our survival and that of our planet Earth," UNESCO director general Koichiro Matsuura said. "No region will be spared from the impact of this crisis, which touches every facet of life, from the health of children to the ability of nations to secure food for their citizens. Water supplies are falling while the demand is dramatically growing at an unsustainable rate. Over the next twenty years, the average supply of water worldwide per person is expected to drop by a third." I'm not big on the UN or on UNESCO, but on this I believe they got it right.

Of course these shortages have given rise to global water funds, which are now a growing investment sector. "The new oil may be water," *Newsweek* reported in August 2007. "According to Global Water Intelligence, a U.K. consultancy, by December [2007] total assets under management in water funds could hit a record $20 billion this year, a 53 percent increase from 12 months earlier. No wonder: since 2001, shares in global water companies have gone up 150 percent. . . . That compares with a 50 percent rise in international blue chips. The reason is simple: there is profit in scarcity. Buffeted by constant news of dying rivers, droughts and water shortages from China to Mexico, investors are increasingly aware that water is a threatened resource."

"If the wars of this century were fought over oil, the wars of the next century will be fought over water," author and World Bank official Ismail Serageldin predicted in 1995. The *Economist* reported: "So is the world running out of the stuff? No, says an American hydrologist Robert Ambroggi: 'The total quantity of fresh water on the Earth exceeds all conceivable needs of the human population.' But tell that to the government of Jordan, which has pumped its underground reserves almost dry since Israel . . . diverted much of its largest water source, the River Jordan. Or to the people of Malta, increasingly dependent on desalinated water since the sea invaded their coastal aquifers. Or to the millions of women in rural Africa walking for hours every day to collect water from polluted wells and muddy riverbeds.

"There is no global water crisis but many severe local water crises."

I'm not trying to come across as a global water expert, but I am an expert on water in four counties in West Texas, where my Mesa Vista Ranch is located. In my experience, oil and water do mix, and I've been involved in both: first, through Mesa Petroleum, and now with Mesa Water. Oil and groundwater share many characteristics. How I went from the former to the latter is quite a story, one with a lesson: there are always new ways of doing things, new opportunities, and better deals.

I grew up in Oklahoma during the Dust Bowl and the Depression, so I've never taken water for granted. For decades, water has been so cheap that too many people have given it little or no value. They consider it a right. I've always been aware that it's a precious resource and is the third-largest global industry after oil and electricity. Water is only going to get more valuable.

Over the past thirty years, the U.S. population has increased 52 percent; in the same period, water consumption has gone up 300 percent, according to a report by the University of Georgia. Just as the world is running out of oil, water is growing scarcer. In 2006, droughts took a toll on Texas. Water restrictions were in force in many areas. The drought might have been a short-term event, but it exposed a long-term problem in a state whose population is expected to double by the year 2040. The water shortage in Texas triggered a new speculative market: securing groundwater. By chance and then by choice, I got involved in the game, which now could turn out to be a $3-billion deal.

It all began on my Mesa Vista Ranch in Roberts County, Texas. I first hunted on what would become the Mesa Vista back in the early 1960s. I hunted quail. The hunting was OK, but the land was dry, arid, and overgrazed. In 1971, I had an opportunity to buy 2,940 acres along the Canadian River. It was the first of many purchases that have grown to become the Mesa Vista Ranch. Now, four decades later, I have 68,000 acres with 24 miles along the Canadian River.

The Canadian River runs through my life. My hometown in Oklahoma, Holdenville, is seven miles north of the Canadian. How do I know that exact figure? Because my Boy Scout troop used to hike from town to the river and back, a total of fourteen miles. That was how we earned one of our merit badges. Follow the river three hundred miles upstream and you come to my Mesa Vista Ranch. For twelve thousand years, the Canadian has been a lifeline for people, from prehistoric man and before. It snakes its way from the highlands of New Mexico, across the Texas Panhandle, and into Oklahoma. My ranch includes twenty-four of the twenty-eight miles of Canadian River frontage in Roberts County. Roberts is one of the least populated counties in Texas, with less than one thousand residents. Long ago it was Apache country, and the Comanches later took control. The Texas Panhandle was also home to Comancheros, a lawless band of outlaws who were gunrunners and slave traffickers.

"Life is cheap up here on the Canadian, and it's likely to get a lot cheaper."

That was one of the many memorable quotes in the Emmy Award-winning miniseries *Lonesome Dove,* which was adapted from Larry McMurtry's Pulitzer Prize-winning novel of the same

name. It's a land with storied history. Even though I've ranched in
Roberts County for thirty-five years, many of my neighbors still consider me a newcomer. Their families have lived there since the
1800s. Roberts County is good ranching country, but the rolling
hills make it ill-suited for farming. The land has important natural
resources: oil, natural gas, water, wind, and wildlife. These resources
are more valuable and more important to the region than farming
or ranching.

When I first bought the land that became the Mesa Vista, the
quail hunting tracked the weather. If it rained, the hunting was
good. If it didn't, the season was nonexistent. I knew we could do
better. All we had to do was provide water, feed, and cover and
undergraze the pastures. The birds would come.

I wanted to make the Mesa Vista the best quail hunting anywhere, and that required water. We put in a seven-mile, four-inch
line. We didn't know if it would do the job or not. It did. We had
abundant quail along that pipeline. When we were through, we put
in fifty miles of water lines. We created a water hole every thousand
feet, over three hundred water holes in all. The birds flourished.
The moisture also created an abundance of bugs, an important food
source for quail chicks. We knew that our water system increased
the quail count. Confirmation of this came even in drought years
when, despite the lack of moisture, our covey size did not go down
but instead remained constant. It was always between twelve and
fifteen birds.

Water was the key to it all. The water was so abundant that
Roberts County was the only place I'd ever been where I couldn't
drill a dry hole. It was no trick getting wells that could pump up to
a thousand gallons a minute. The reason for this abundance? The
Ogallala aquifer.

Land in Roberts County that was once cheap isn't cheap anymore, and wind and water are playing a part in that increase in
value. The Ogallala is one of the largest aquifers in the United
States. It is a vast reservoir and contains an estimated three billion
acre-feet of beautiful, clean water. It's said that this aquifer could
cover all of the fifty states with 14.5 inches of water. The Ogallala
covers 174,000 square miles beneath South Dakota, Nebraska,
Wyoming, Colorado, Kansas, Oklahoma, New Mexico, and the Texas
Panhandle, including my Mesa Vista Ranch.

I had cattle on the ranch, but I discovered that I wasn't a cattle-
man. Cattlemen love to go out and look at their cattle, which bores
the hell out of me. I'd rather go look at wildlife. I laugh at myself
in a cowboy hat. I'm just a quail hunter from Oklahoma.

I fell in love with Roberts County. It's where I call home. The first
house on the ranch—the Reynolds home place—was built over
a century ago in 1903. Not far from there, my original home at
217 North Kelker, which was built by my grandfather for my parents in 1923, was trucked over from Holdenville, a surprise birth-
day gift from Madeleine.

Four years ago, I decided I wanted to build a unique home that
blended into the landscape. It took three years to build. It's surrounded by lakes and boasts the best bass fishing in the world. It's
the work of Tommy Ford, my contractor, and Tommy Roberts, my
architect. Together we've built nine houses over the years. We
weren't constrained by money—only by our imaginations. I'm convinced it is one of the most distinctive houses on any ranch anywhere. Made of rock and stone, it will be there forever. I'll be real
surprised if there are any changes ever made to it. It's that perfect.

I honestly cannot tell you how much I enjoy being on my
ranch. I've given serious thought to living in Roberts County and

commuting to Dallas. It's such a part of my life that I've commissioned a coffee table book about it, which is currently being produced by my good friend Bubba Wood at Collector's Covey in Dallas (www.collectorscovey.com).

Bubba and I go way back. A champion wingshot, he is also a dedicated steward of the land. Whenever we take a tour of the ranch, he ticks off the names of the ducks that take flight—bluewing teal, ring-necks, buffleheads, widgeons, mallards, gadwalls, canvasbacks. The list is endless.

Bubba enlisted the services of Ray Sasser and Wyman Meinzer to produce *Mesa Vista.* Ray is a Texas institution. He's been on staff at the *Dallas Morning News* for thirty years and is without question the dean of outdoor writers in the state. Wyman's credentials are equally impressive. In 1997, the Texas legislature named him state photographer. Bubba describes him this way: "Wyman is what everyone thinks a Texan should be, and he's what every Texan wants to be." He's made the drive up from Benjamin to the Mesa Vista to photograph all aspects of the ranch, from its natural beauty to the countless improvements we have made over the years.

We've brought in over four thousand semitrailer loads of material. Line those semis up bumper to bumper and they would stretch fifty-one miles. During the height of construction, there were nearly two hundred workers on site. Landscaping included the purchase of more than ten thousand mature trees: sycamores, cottonwoods, pines, pears, lilacs. We had them freighted in from Colorado, Illinois, Tennessee, and Timbuktu. You name it, we got it. The house is surrounded by acres of water—ponds, aqueducts, waterfalls, all of which contrast with the arid land. I thought the most valuable resource on the ranch was wildlife—mule deer and whitetailed deer, pronghorn antelope, turkey, pheasant, and blue and bobwhite quail—but by the 1990s it became clear to me that the water was equally, if not more, valuable.

Let me give you some background on Texas water law. If you own the land, you own what's beneath it. That's not that way it is in every state. There is no unregulated pumping of groundwater; that is regulated by local groundwater conservation districts. Water is pumped out of the Ogallala daily for agricultural purposes. But the four counties that make up our water project are 95 percent ranch land. The terrain is largely rolling hills, making it unsuitable for farming. In the counties to the west and south of us, however, people rely on irrigation from the aquifer. In our four counties, ranchers use less than 10 percent of the water for ranching. The rest of the water is just sitting untapped and unused.

The Ogallala aquifer holds more high-quality water than all the landowners in Roberts County could ever use. The rest of Texas is not so lucky. In the summer of 2006, Texas had one of its worst droughts on record. So much of the state was plagued by so little rain that Governor Rick Perry eventually declared a statewide disaster. North Texas had one of its driest years since the 1950s. Several reservoirs that supply Dallas drinking water were approaching all-time lows. The drought and record heat resulted in fires across 3.7 million acres statewide, including an 840,000-acre burn in the Panhandle, the largest wildfire in the history of the state. It destroyed four hundred homes and killed eleven people.

Reservoirs are seen as the solution to the state's increasing water needs. Dallas suffered through a seven-year drought in the 1950s, and responded by building man-made reservoirs to supply the area's water. Many of these were going dry in the summer of 2006. Plans are being made to build new reservoirs to help solve the water shortages, including the long-planned Marvin Nichols

Reservoir in East Texas, but building a new reservoir is a thirty-year proposition at best. Texas needs the water now.

One way to address this issue is to tap into the aquifer beneath the land of the four counties in the northeast corner of the Panhandle. Before 1997, nobody had done anything about trying to sell their water. We coined a phrase to describe our water: stranded and surplus.

I did not realize the value of our water until 1997, when I read in the newspaper that the Canadian River Municipal Water Authority (CRMWA) was buying 43,000 acres of water rights from the Southwestern Public Service Company for $349 an acre. The price astounded me. So I called CRMWA.

"I've got water that joins you on the north," I said. "Are you interested in buying any of that?" I was at a point where I needed money. It was apparent that they had no interest in my water. That was a big mistake on their part. They should have bought my water and put me to bed.

Salem Abraham is a friend from adjacent Hemphill County. Salem, whose family goes back several generations in his hometown of Canadian, told me that he and his brothers were getting into the water business. They had obtained 71,000 acres of water rights, which was three times as much as I had. We started to put our heads together.

Salem said, "Boone, why don't we throw in together? You've got twenty-five thousand acres. Your three neighbors control another twenty thousand. So that's a forty-five-thousand-acre package. If we added our seventy-one thousand acres, we'd have nearly one hundred and twenty thousand acres."

That sounded like a good plan to me. At first, anyway. We had to work out the details, and that took some haggling. After several meetings, we almost hammered out a deal. There was one sticking point: how would we split it up? We never could figure that out.

In 1999, Salem netted $10 million by selling his water rights to Amarillo for $20 million, or $264 an acre. Soon after Salem called to tell me about the sale, I was on a trip to Austin when I bumped into Fran Morrison, my neighbor in Roberts County, who had been in on Salem's deal.

"Boone, I want to tell you how much I appreciate your help in the sale of our water," she said. "Really appreciate it, because we needed to make the sale."

"I didn't have anything to do with the sale."

"Yes, you did. We give you credit for the sale."

Salem had told Amarillo that they had better buy his water, and if they didn't he was going to join forces with me and sell our water to Fort Worth. "We're not doing a deal with Boone, and if Boone's water is in the deal, we're not doing it," the city manager had told Salem.

I called Salem and asked him over to lunch a week or so later.

"I feel like you kind of used me on that water deal you cut with Amarillo," I said.

"What do you mean?"

"Well, you know, I heard that you told them that if they didn't buy your water, you were going to partner with me and sell it to Fort Worth."

"No, I didn't exactly say that," he replied.

"Well, I feel like you used me."

He laughed. "Well, you did come in handy."

After Salem sold his water, I wrote Amarillo and offered to sell them my water. I knew they would turn me down, but I wanted it in writing. They had a chance to buy my water and take me out of the water business. Just like CRMWA, they let it slip through their fingers. Six years later the tables would turn when Amarillo and CRMWA offered to buy me out with a nice profit. It was my turn to tell them, "Don't call me. I'll call you." To this day, Salem and his brothers are the only ones who have brokered any water sale in Roberts County.

In 2000, eleven landowners filed applications with the Panhandle Groundwater Conservation District for permits to produce our water. We didn't have a buyer, but we wanted to be cleared to sell if we found one. It took two years, but we finally got our permits and were ready to market water. All we were missing was a buyer. Our opportunities for a sale were downstate, to either Dallas/Fort Worth or San Antonio. Our engineers came up with a plan for a 328-mile pipeline running from Roberts County to North Texas. It would be an underground pipeline with a diameter of nine feet, big enough to drive a car through. Some critics claim that we'll drain the Ogallala. I won't let that happen. We have proposed and supported regulations that ensure that the aquifer is never drawn down more than 50 percent. Remember, it's surplus water we're selling.

The next major step took place at a dinner I had with Bobby Stillwell at the Mesa Vista Ranch. It was in January 2006, and we had just seen record-setting returns in both our energy and our equity funds. During dinner and afterward, we covered a lot of subjects, and water was one of the most important ones.

"We've made enough money this year," Bobby said. "Let's go ahead and put some in water. It will certainly show our commitment to the project."

So we did. Shortly afterward we made an offer to our neighbors to buy 50 percent of their water for up to $500 an acre. This would increase the value of their property substantially and allow them to get even more when they sold the remaining 50 percent.

The *Canadian Record* noted that our project has "led to a tremendous increase in local land values." Since we started, land values in Roberts and Hemphill counties have increased from $200 to $700 per acre. I don't mind taking credit for adding this value. The acquisition of water rights by Amarillo, CRMWA, and Mesa Water will lead to a huge transfer of wealth: $90 to $100 million to fewer than one hundred families in these two counties. For my part I've never taken a dime out of Roberts County, and my total investment in water—rights, fees, and other costs—exceeds $100 million.

Our water project will turn out to be an example of how the private sector can move more quickly, efficiently, and creatively than the public sector. We can deliver water faster and more cheaply than any other option on the table. Our water is terrorist-proof and drought-proof and can be brought to market at least a quarter century before a new reservoir can be built. I am confident that I am the largest owner of permitted groundwater in the United States.

This project is not a question of if but when, and I'm betting it's soon.

CHAPTER 12

The Biggest Deal of My Career: Wind

Booneism #27: *Action leads to more action.*

THIS IS SOMETHING I've discovered in my business career. It's happened many times. I've started with an idea that I think is a good one, and that idea will put me in a direction that points toward a deal. What happens is that before I get to the conclusion of the first deal, I'll come up with another idea along the way that is even better than the first one.

Our water project is a prime example of this. It has doubled in size and is now a $3-billion venture with a lot of interesting angles. It's a deal that should be done, because you can't leave a valuable asset stranded. It is incumbent on me to see that everybody gets a kiss at the pig. But we're going to have to work on it. Meanwhile our neighbors across the fence, CRMWA, are slowly draining us with their wells. They can do it. That's the law. The only thing we can do about it is find a buyer and start producing and selling our water. Mesa Water will require an investment in both time and money for many years to come, yet our water deal is already paying off because it's led us to the Big Kahuna: wind.

Wind is a $10-billion project. It's easier than water. It's bigger than water. Best of all, it complements water. It's already increasing the value of our Roberts County holdings. If you can stand the appearance of turbines, this is going to be a great way to make money. Developing water and wind in a rural area in the Texas Panhandle has spurred a huge enhancement of land and land values, and the small city of Pampa will become the wind capital of the Texas Panhandle.

Word of my intentions quickly hit the street, as evidenced by this June 2007 article in the *Fort Worth Star-Telegram:*

> In the late 1980s and early 1990s, Boone Pickens lost much of his hard-won fortune by investing heavily in natural gas properties. When gas prices failed to rise as expected, he took a humongous hit to the wallet.
>
> The wealthy Dallas oilman and investor wants to build the world's largest wind farm in the Texas Panhandle. . . .
>
> Pickens's proposed new energy gamble is important to Texas because it could put the state another significant step toward reducing its heavy reliance on fossil fuels for electricity generation. It also could help solidify Texas's number-one ranking among the 50 states in wind power generation capacity.
>
> Never accused of thinking small, Pickens could put as many as 2,000 wind turbines on nearly 200,000 acres in thinly populated Gray, Roberts, Hemphill and Wheeler counties. He's talking about generating 2,000 to 4,000 megawatts of electricity, roughly the equivalent of one or two Comanche Peak nuclear power plants. . . .

Booneism #28: *Everything here happens fast. There isn't any standing around or looking at your watch.*

I DIDN'T HAVE to look for the wind project.

The wind deal found me, just like the water deal found me by CRMWA's actions.

Wind hasn't always been considered a potential resource of alternative and clean energy. Alternative forms of energy come into their own not merely because of necessity but because they become economically viable. As the price of oil gets higher, everything gets a chance.

Wind is clean, readily available, domestic, and a renewable natural resource. According to various sources, it's one of the oldest forms of energy and dates back to ancient Persia, where wind contraptions were used to grind grain. It wasn't until 1887 that the first windmill was used for electricity production. That happened in Scotland and was followed that same year with a more substantial version built in Cleveland by a local engineer. By the 1890s, Denmark was already using windmills for electrical generation. In 1980, twenty turbines were arrayed en masse in New Hampshire to create the first wind farm. In 1981, a wind farm on Altamont Pass in California became the world's largest until "it fizzled, largely because of low natural-gas prices that made renewable energy sources noncompetitive," according to the *Los Angeles Times.*

The *Times* also quoted a 2005 Stanford University study that showed there is "enough wind worldwide to satisfy global electricity demand seven times over, even if only 20 percent of the power could be captured." Germany and Spain are two of the world's leaders in wind energy. Thanks to its wide-open spaces, Texas is the national leader in wind power development, with almost twice as much current generating capacity as California, which ranks second. All told, forty-six states have sufficient winds to produce commercial wind power. One study by the American Wind Association showed that "North Dakota alone could supply about one-third of the nation's electricity." Texas can produce 98 percent of what North Dakota can produce.

The United States lags behind the rest of the world in wind development. Denmark already has 21.3 percent of its power demand satisfied by wind. In this country, that figure was less than 1 percent in 2007, when 14,491 turbines generated 16,181 megawatts of electricity (10,000 megawatts is enough to power over 2.6 million homes).

We look at the problems Third World countries face, and we have great sympathy for them. They should have sympathy for us. We have done an absolutely pitiful job taking care of our energy needs. As my dad said one time, "Son, it looks like you've worked this deal around so that you've got them by your balls." That's exactly where we are. Why are we, the world's most advanced nation in so many respects, so backward when it comes to energy? I can tell you why: lack of leadership. Because we keep doing nothing and acting like everything will be fine. An example of what I'm talking about is the way that every presidential candidate promises energy independence upon their election and then does nothing.

When it comes to wind power, Texas is an exception to the rule and has experienced rapid development of wind energy over the past decade, thanks in part to legislation signed into law by Governor George W. Bush. In 1999, the state legislature established the goal of developing 2,000 megawatts of renewable energy capacity by 2009. Texas is well ahead of this target and already has wind energy facilities capable of producing more than 4,300 mega-watts. The state's current goal is to have 10,000 megawatts of re-newable generation capacity by 2025. I am confident that we will achieve this goal. I never understood why President Bush did not promote wind energy during his administration as he did in Texas.

Texas has opened the door for developers and landowners to make money from wind. Not only does the state have a pro-business environment, but also many of its landowners possess an entrepreneurial spirit and have developed revenue streams from activities such as hunting and ecotourism. Seeking new forms of alternative power, the legislature directed the Public Utility Com-mission to identify prime areas for wind energy development that weren't close to existing transmission lines. One of those areas was just south of my Mesa Vista Ranch in Roberts County.

The wind blows almost all the time in the Texas Panhandle. It's part of the landscape. In winter, the wind comes fast and cold in the form of blue northers that hang icicles off the cattle's noses. It's exhilarating to be outside in this high, dry climate. The wind in the Texas Panhandle is rated Class 4. With an average wind speed of 16.8 miles per hour at a height of 164 feet, it is ideal for power gen-eration. There are several other advantages to developing wind energy, including proximity to load, ease of access, and flat terrain for construction. Add these to the area's great expanses of land and its motivated landowners, and there couldn't be a better place to erect a major wind farm. The only downside to wind is the turbines themselves. None are going to be placed on my ranch, but if the looks of them don't bother you, it's a hell of a deal. They are just like oil wells but with no pollution and no decline curve.

Selling wind might seem like a strange concept, but there's a wind boom occurring in Texas not dissimilar to the oil booms of the past. When oil is discovered, oilmen lease a landowner's mineral rights to drill a well. The landowner receives a royalty for the oil extracted. The same thing is true for landowners in the wind business, except they get royalties for a resource that is above their land instead of beneath it. Best of all, there are no dry holes and it never depletes. Landowners lease developers their land on which to erect wind turbines, which can measure up to 330 feet tall from the ground to the hub—the center of the blades—and another 150 feet or more from the hub to the tips of the blades. A wind turbine this size is the equivalent of a 48-story building. The turbine generates electricity, which travels through an underground transmission line and then collects in a transformer substation. Most of today's turbines generate one to three megawatts of power, enough for anywhere from 260 to 790 homes, depending on the size of the turbine and the average wind speed. The power will be channeled through transmission lines to houses and industry wherever electricity is needed.

Wind developers, including Shell, Florida Power, and Babcock & Brown, an Australian company, had already started leasing land in the Panhandle by the time I got into the game. We had looked into the wind business about four years earlier and decided the time wasn't right. Before I jumped into wind, I did what I always do: I hired the best consultants and commissioned a feasibility study. We immediately found enough data to reach some conclusions. First, the resource is there. The wind is excellent, blowing at high velocity for long periods of time with few calm days. Second, where we are still looking for a buyer for our water, there are already plenty of buyers for the wind power.

As things progressed, my often-invoked axiom that action leads to more action and one deal leads to even bigger and better deals became extremely evident. In our office, we have what I call very good "deal flow." There's tremendous combined knowledge within our close-knit group. We were in the conference room one day, looking at how the prime wind area was almost an overlay to our water deal, and a couple of things stood out: we have one of the best wind areas in the United States; and we could put the wind power transmission line along the same right-of-way as the water pipeline.

After the preliminary study, we embarked on a series of steps we call "go, no-go." Each succeeding step has a higher level of certainty regarding the potential success of the project. Not surprisingly, every subsequent step costs more. Our consultants were in the field, gathering more information, doing heavy design work, and constructing meteorological towers that measure what the wind is doing over our prospect area twenty-four hours a day. Every step led us to believe that we had a "go" project.

The annual rate of return on this $10 billion investment would be a minimum of 15 percent on equity. The first 1,000 megawatts of our project would come online in 2011. And since wind is a renewable energy source, it will always exist.

"OK, let's go to the next step," I told our consultants, meaning additional studies and more money. Mesa Power, LP, was born.

With our plans in place, the next step was to buy leases from the landowners on whose land we would be erecting turbines. In February 2007, we had the first of several meetings with landowners. Since Pampa is the epicenter of the Panhandle's wind industry, we did it at the Pampa Country Club. About 125 people showed up. Many of them were elderly, but there were plenty of young people determined to keep their family land intact. I knew many of them from our water deal. All were friends and neighbors.

"If you want to sell your wind, I want you to know that the best deal is going to come from me," I told the audience. "Some of you are part of our water deal, and I told you we were going to increase the value of your land from two hundred dollars an acre to seven hundred dollars," I said. "That has happened, and I have now spent over $100 million and still haven't gotten a buyer for the water." That got a laugh.

Later in the year we had a second meeting, this time at the Pampa Convention Center. This time more than two hundred people showed up. I greeted them with this comment: "I want everybody to know that I do not want wind turbines on my property."

From the back of the room, Katie Wilde yelled, "Why don't you want 'em, Boone?"

"Because they're ugly."

Then a guy in the front row yelled out, "I don't see that well. They may be ugly to Boone, but they look like money to me!" Another big laugh.

Wind energy was an easy sell; the Panhandle is famous for being windy. Most of the landowners, when they hear about what they can make in royalty income, get interested quick. A 640-acre section of land can support five to ten wind turbines. Each turbine can generate $10,000 to $30,000 in royalties annually. Depending on the size of your land and the number of turbines, you could get rich. And windmills don't interfere with land use either. We're leasing turbine sites for thirty years with two ten-year extensions. We expect the wind farm to generate electricity forever.

By early 2008, we had already leased 300,000 acres, and we expect to lease another 100,000 acres. Our wind farm will stretch over five counties—Carson, Gray, Hemphill, Roberts, and Wheeler—

with Pampa at its center. Right now the local economy is based on farming, ranching, and oil and gas. In 1990, the population of this five-county area was 40,871. While the state of Texas grew by more than 30 percent over the following fifteen years, this area declined almost 10 percent in population, to 37,127. Young people were migrating to larger cities. The job base was evaporating. Like so many rural areas across America, these counties are desperately in need of economic development to reverse the decline that has taken place over the last several decades. Not only will there be significant increases in jobs and income in the five counties where our wind farms are located, but the economy of this part of Texas will be radically enhanced as well. I'm certain it's going to boost economic growth in this area beyond any other project on the horizon, and it could be a model for a much larger project, one that is national in scope.

Although we've had enormous interest from people eager to become part of our deal, I have no partners at this point. I know it will work, but I also know I don't have $10 billion to finance the entire project. I see the wind deal as a 100-yard track with ten hurdles on it. I figure I can get over three or four hurdles without having a partner. The farther I get down that track solo, the greater the potential upside. I never stop thinking like an entrepreneur.

Wind will be the biggest deal of my career, and that includes Gulf Oil. My ultimate vision is to see the Texas Panhandle restored to pristine prairie, with a recovery of the lesser prairie chicken, and an abundance of pheasant, quail, turkey, antelope, and deer. It can be an unbelievable paradise for wildlife. My pristine prairie project has the potential to be even larger than wind, and it will get under way when I get wind and water over a few more hurdles. Wind and water will make this region unique in America for decades to come. People say I'm becoming a one-man chamber of commerce for the area. I don't argue.

My friend and neighbor across the Canadian River is Harold Courson. He has a 64,000-acre ranch. Along with mine, our ranches spread over more than 25 percent of Roberts County. Like me, Courson went to Oklahoma State. Both our fathers worked for Phillips Petroleum. We're both only children. One night over dinner, I told Courson that Mesa Vista would eventually be one of the most valuable properties in Texas. "You'll think I'm crazy when I tell you what I believe it will be worth," I said.

Courson laughed. "Boone, up here we all used to think you were crazy," he said. "But we don't anymore."

CHAPTER 13

The Big Idea: An Energy
Plan for America

Booneism #29: *A fool with a plan can outsmart a genius with no plan any day.*

I'VE TALKED ABOUT a lot of things in the previous twelve chapters, describing key events in my life and offering observations on business. But this chapter is dead serious. It's the most important one in the book. It has the potential to break every dish in the kitchen.

Let me begin by saying that I'm a big fan of President Ronald Reagan. I am positive he will go down as one of the greatest leaders in American history. I was an avid supporter in both of his presidential campaigns, and I've given $35 million to the Ronald Reagan Presidential Library. I'm sure I'll give more. Whether you loved President Reagan as I did or you didn't, you have to admire his accomplishments. He won the Cold War and brought down the Berlin Wall. Not a single bullet was fired. Not a single life lost. How did he do it? By leadership. He bankrupted the Soviet economy. He outspent the Red Army, and in their attempt to keep pace, the Politburo crippled the Soviet economy and hastened its collapse.

Can the same thing happen to us? Are we crippling our economy? We're definitely an easy target. If we don't get a grip on our foreign oil dependence and rein in this spending, our economy will suffer irreparable damage. Perhaps even more important, our status as a superpower will be jeopardized. It's time to declare war on a crisis that threatens the very security of America by sending close to $1 trillion overseas each year, enriching our enemies, downgrading our global status, and pushing our already fragile financial condition toward almost certain meltdown.

We have to act, not just create policy. Decisions need to be made now. When it comes to energy, we are at war. You don't think so? Perhaps these words will ring a bell:

"Our decision about energy will test the character of the American people and the ability of the president and the Congress to govern. This difficult effort will be the moral equivalent of war, except that we will be uniting our efforts to build and not destroy."

More than thirty years ago, President Carter delivered these remarks to the nation in a nationally televised address. Jimmy Carter is no Ronald Reagan, but on this point I agree with him 100 percent. We must develop an energy plan, one complete with leadership, money, timetables, and, most important, immediate action to get us through what I am convinced is the darkest threat facing this country in the twenty-first century. If the American people understand what we're up against, I'm confident that we can solve the problem. We have to set goals, monitor the progress, and report to the public. It's everybody's problem, and everyone can be a part of the solution.

Each month foreign oil costs us several times what we are

spending to fight the Iraq war. Have you ever heard someone say this before? Have you ever seen a senator or a congressman take the floor with these figures? I haven't, and that bothers me. Right now we're spending almost $50 billion a month on imported oil, while the war in Iraq, which former Federal Reserve Chairman Alan Greenspan famously described as "largely about oil," is costing us $12 billion a month, or 25 percent the cost of imported oil. In 2008, Bloomberg forecasts that OPEC will receive almost $1 trillion in net oil-export revenue from oil-importing countries such as the United States. Over the next decade, oil imports are expected to cost us more than $6 trillion, and that's at $100 a barrel. I'd give three-to-one odds that it will be closer to $10 trillion. That's money we don't have, and certainly not money we can afford to send to countries that hate us.

People frequently ask me, "What would you do about the energy crisis if you were secretary of energy?" I wouldn't take the job. Too much bureaucracy. We need to create a more authoritative position: energy czar best describes it. The energy czar would be empowered to be decisive, to act fast, and to fix this problem. In times of war, the president is given emergency powers to act without interference. This is what we desperately need right now: leadership whose mandate is to make reducing America's reliance on foreign oil our number one national priority.

First, we must identify the domestic resources we have to work with: coal, natural gas, nuclear, wind, and solar, as well as our limited oil reserves. Other miscellaneous fuels can fill in, too. We must begin to develop these energy sources immediately and take that power to market, bringing the best energy to our country. Specific methods for implementing policy—taxes, incentives, securing transmission line right-of-ways, and development standards—must be determined immediately. To many, the case for alternative fuels is about cleaning up the environment. For me, the primary case for alternative energy is to help America achieve its national energy security. As long as we are dependent on other countries for oil, the very lifeblood of our nation, our security is at risk.

Where am I headed with this?

Action leads to more action. One deal leads to another deal.

Just as water led me to wind, wind has led me to the development of a national energy plan. Since 75 percent of the oil we import goes to transportation, shifting natural gas away from power generation and into transportation would be a key step to reducing our dependency on imported oil. Installed electrical generating capacity in the United States is approaching 1 million megawatts annually. Projections show that in the next ten years we're going to need an additional 150,000 megawatts, a 15 percent increase. If you look at the pie chart of current power generation in America, it's approximately 50 percent coal, 20 percent nuclear, and 22 percent natural gas. The remainder is primarily hydroelectric, in addition to renewables. Natural gas has become the fuel of choice for power generation because coal is a dirty word. The problem with this trend is the fact that of the principal sources of power generation, natural gas is the highest priced.

We don't have many options: clean up coal, move natural gas into transportation, open up ANWR, and develop renewable sources. I've taken a close look at the potential for wind energy—first as an investment, and more recently as a possible solution to our current energy woes. I give it high marks on both counts. The Wind Belt, the enormous corridor that extends the length of the Great Plains from Texas to the Canadian border east of the Rockies, is ideal for building wind farms. From a security standpoint, it's also the most secure place for a mega-billion-dollar project of this magnitude. Remote and distant from both coastlines, this thousand-mile renewable energy corridor runs through the heartland of our country. The residents within this corridor would embrace such a proposal because of the many benefits it would bring them. A second corridor, one devoted to both wind and solar energy, needs to be established on an east-west axis from Texas to California. This is our country's prime solar belt, and to a lesser extent we could also develop wind energy in this corridor.

Solar and wind will require government subsidies. This is a chance for Congress to show some leadership. I would much rather subsidize solar and wind than spend billions on foreign oil, wouldn't you? Each energy corridor will also require a dedicated transmission component; those right-of-ways need to be secured through congressional action. Government will have to lead the way. Wind and solar projects are eligible for federal production tax credits, but there is continued uncertainty about whether Congress will regularly renew these credits. Investors will need long-term assurances before committing the huge dollars to develop these corridors. Because of the urgency of the problem, they can't be micromanaged by Congress or bureaucrats. This has to be a team effort. Remember, we're talking about the moral equivalent of war. Speed is of the essence.

We need to approach this just as President Eisenhower declared an emergency during the Cold War to create the interstate highway system. Something similar to his approach could be used here to develop the transmission corridors. The Department of Energy recently announced a plan whereby we could use wind to generate 20 percent of our electricity. I agree with the plan, but I disagree with the timing. Their projected year for this to be implemented is 2030. The country will be bankrupt if it takes that long. We have to make the transition in less than ten years.

One 3-megawatt wind turbine can produce the same amount of energy in a year as 12,000 barrels of imported oil. Unlike oil, there is no shortage of wind in our nation's Wind Belt, or of sun in the Southwest. If transmission lines were built to support the wind and solar corridors I'm proposing, there would be enough wind and solar power to generate 20 to 40 percent of the nation's electricity. Natural gas and clean coal would be included to meet our daily electric demand when wind and solar power would not suffice. These two national energy corridors could solve a great deal of America's problems and release natural gas for transportation. This is vital.

I'll say it again: the federal government must mandate the transmission corridors required to the East and West coasts. In addition, these two energy corridors are in the perfect location. They need massive economic revitalization. The small West Texas community of Sweetwater is a good example. Best known for its annual Rattlesnake Roundup, it now bills itself as the Wind Energy Capital. The world's largest wind farm, Horse Hollow, is located just outside this town of twelve thousand. With the wind farm came jobs and with the jobs came people. Sweetwater has now turned into a boomtown. When you look at the positives that have happened, you can see that Sweetwater is a model for small towns and rural communities throughout these two corridors, where my adage of "resurgence instead of retirement" could be applied on a national scale. Landowners would reap royalties from the renewable energies produced on their property. Farms and ranches would become more profitable.

I can only imagine the changes our wind farm in West Texas will bring to Pampa. This community of close to twenty thousand will be at the center of a wind farm six times bigger than Horse Hollow and supplying 4,000 megawatts. Our section of the rural Texas Panhandle will enjoy an unprecedented economic boom, and Pampa will benefit in many ways: job growth, housing construction, and a larger tax base. In the decades to come, I see this happening to countless communities like Sweetwater and Pampa.

Over the next fifty years the United States is going to need much more wind, solar, and other alternative energy. We have to get into these businesses. There's no way we can generate the energy we need the way we're doing things today. The future is in renewables. We need a visionary step forward. We need leadership to say, "This is what we must do to win the war against foreign oil and end our dangerous and fatal addiction. Here's a new idea. A bold idea." We need more than a movement. We need someone to effectively and decisively lead us through this war. I'm convinced the times require a George Patton, someone who can lead us to victory no matter the obstacles. Here are some of my ideas on how to increase production of domestic forms of energy.

MOVE NATURAL GAS OUT OF POWER GENERATION AND INTO TRANSPORTATION

This is without question the most critical move we have to make. Natural gas is our country's second-largest energy resource. Only our coal reserves surpass it. Recent advances now make it possible to produce enormous amounts of gas from carboniferous shales in fields such as the Barnett, located in North Texas. Aubrey McClendon at Chesapeake Energy says there are nineteen potential shale plays in the United States, and we are only producing from four of them. The potential production from these shales is huge and will guarantee that our country has all the natural gas it needs for decades to come. By finding new means of power generation—clean coal, increased nuclear, wind, and solar—we can shift natural gas to transportation. *How do you replace the natural gas currently being used for power generation?* You replace it with wind and solar. All of this would allow natural gas to move into its higher value role as a vehicular fuel, a second infrastructure to gasoline and diesel, allowing us to reduce our need to import crude oil. And remember, natural gas will always be cheaper than gasoline and diesel. I'll bet my ass on this one. Just as important, gasoline and diesel are imported; our natural gas is sourced domestically, and there is plenty of natural gas for both power generation and transportation. This resource is our salvation. It must not be ignored.

CLEAN UP COAL

Right now we need energy that we can get quickly and easily. Coal is the answer. It is our number one natural resource. When you look at the present power-generation pie chart of coal, nuclear, and natural gas, 50 percent of it is coal. We're already using a lot. We know it works. However, coal is far from clean. Not long ago, TXU, the big Texas-based utility, announced plans to construct eleven coal-fired plants. Most were killed after a lengthy series of public hearings and a barrage of complaints from citizens, environmentalists, and municipalities. This sentiment has spread to other parts of the country; other coal projects have been canceled. People don't want dirty coal.

As soon as I say, "We have to expand the nuke and clean up the coal," somebody typically interrupts me and says, "Pickens, you say that real quick. Do you have a plan for cleaning up coal?" I do not.

That's not my business. Still, you can't tell me it can't be done. We have to use what we have available. Anything is better than importing foreign oil.

STEP UP NUCLEAR POWER

Many people are against nuclear power. Well, we're going to have to have nuclear if we're going to solve this problem. We know it works. We have to renew and expand America's nuclear power industry. It's happening around the world. China and Japan are both ahead of us in nuclear, and so is France, where 80 percent of electrical power is nuclear generated. Compare that figure with the 20 percent generated in the United States. Nuclear power generation is about one-third the cost of natural gas power generation. I realize nuclear power has a bad reputation in the United States. Get over it. This is war.

Nuclear accidents are rare. Nobody's ever been killed in this country by one. More nuclear is coming, not because we want it but because we have to have it. Right now it takes at least ten years before a new nuclear plant can go online in the United States. No matter what the critics say, nuclear beats the hell out of foreign oil. We have to fast-track this; ten years is too long.

I REALIZE THESE CHANGES cannot happen overnight. The plan must include a transition period to alternative energy. The first step is to kill demand for gasoline. A gas tax may be the way to go. I'm not running for office, so I can say things like that. I'm also not a tax expert, but I do know this tax would hurt some and that we'd have to offset this with deductions or tax decreases elsewhere. Let the experts figure this one out. These changes must be made in order to achieve national energy security. If everybody understands the plan, then everybody cooperates. We need leaders who understand and know what we have to do.

Don't even consider subsidizing energy. Making it cheap only makes it that much easier to waste. Another thing that won't work is a windfall profits tax. It makes no sense to penalize energy companies for making money that they can use to develop new sources of energy. A windfall profits tax would also be a disaster because it taxes stockholders, and more than half the population in America are stockholders. We have to clear the deck and cut out the silly rhetoric. All it does is confuse the situation.

While Europe is as dependent on oil as we are, they came up with a plan. They got nuclear and wind while we wasted our time on empty energy policies. Our present policy is: Here's our money. Send more oil. Imagine if we had developed a realistic energy plan, as France did twenty years ago. We wouldn't be in this bind. Imagine how different we'd look. Too late now. That's what happens when you don't have leadership.

I lay awake nights worrying about our increasingly fatal addiction to foreign oil. Imagine the ways we could invest the $1 trillion we spend on imported oil each year if we invested it on wind energy.

We could:

- Build 235,000 megawatts of wind generation and associated transmission

- Increase U.S. renewable power generation twelve times, to 24 percent of installed capacity

- Replace 90 percent of natural gas currently used for power generation

- Replace 36 percent of gasoline demand with natural gas

- Lower our foreign oil bill by $120 billion (about 16 percent) a
  year and greatly reduce our dependence and vulnerability

This is no silver bullet that solves the problem, but my national
energy plan beats anything we've seen yet. The most important
thing that might come of it is that all Americans realize what we're
up against. With that understanding comes conservation, which
could be a huge factor in developing our energy security. Once
everybody gets on board, there will be all kinds of things happening that will save us.

The national energy plan I'm proposing must be implemented
as quickly as possible. In the short term, nothing can change the
fact that we're addicted to oil. Fifty years from now, a high percentage of our energy will come from alternative sources. The hydrocarbon era began with the automobile in 1900. One hundred years
from now, I'm convinced the hydrocarbon era will be over. Not all
of the hydrocarbons will be gone, but we will have made the switch
to other forms of energy for transportation.

I've heard suggestions of a Manhattan Project–like energy con-
vocation where leaders in the industry try to find real solutions to
our problems, just as we did when America marshaled its brainpower during World War II. I can tell you just how that would probably turn out: not one damn thing would come out of it except
more policies, more papers, more talk, and no action. I'll say it
again: it all comes down to leadership. We've got to find the leadership to make things happen. Ending the energy crisis is going to
take nothing less than a declaration of war. It must begin now.

If it doesn't, if we don't get some leadership and take action, I'm
afraid we're going to continue spending $1 trillion or more year

after year on foreign oil. And when the sellers of the oil have taken our money, we will have transferred a tremendous part of our wealth to them in order to burn up their fuel in our cars. Those countries, knowing they have a finite resource, will arrogantly tell us they have to cut back on their oil sales to protect their reserves for future generations and that they have a responsibility to control our insatiable, exorbitant demand for oil. Oil prices will go even higher, and we will eventually be reduced from a superpower to something else.

God only knows what that might be.

Afterword: Going Forward

Booneism #30: Show up early. Work hard. Stay late. Work eight hours and sleep eight hours, and make sure that they are not the same eight hours.

IT GOES WITHOUT saying that the national energy plan I've proposed is not for me; it's for the generations to come. That was what was on my mind last summer as I gave the commencement address to the graduating class at St. Stephen's & St. Agnes School in Alexandria, Virginia. My grandson Alexander Cordia was a member of the class of 2007, and as I stood before Alexander and the rest of the graduating seniors I told them that I already knew what was on their minds:

When is this guy going to stop talking so we can go have lunch?

But first we had some business to take care of. "Before we go to lunch, I want to make you a thought-provoking offer," I said. "I hope you realize where you are in life today. You have the best seat in the house. I would trade you everything I have for it."

Boy, things got serious quick.

"My Gulfstream airplane. My sixty-eight-thousand-acre ranch." I ticked off a long list of my assets before adding, "I would gladly give it all to any one of you to be where you are sitting right now. There's only one catch. If you make the trade, you have to be seventy-nine and I get to be eighteen again."

Suddenly, lunch didn't seem that important after all. They were trying to figure out how to get what I had without giving me what I wanted. Guess who had gotten their attention? After I finished my speech, two of Alexander's classmates came up to me and said, "You really got us thinking today, Mr. Pickens."

"You guys want to make the trade?"

First these fellows needed to do some due diligence.

"Is the Gulfstream a 550?"

"Sure is."

"How big are the deer on your ranch?"

"Some of the biggest in the Panhandle. And the quail hunting is the best in the world."

Although I did my best to answer their questions, in the end I got no takers. They all decided that no amount of wealth could persuade them to change places with a man about to turn eighty. "We'd miss everything between eighteen and seventy-nine if we changed places with you," one said.

The truth is it was a bad deal . . . for them. I would have traded it all for another shot at eighteen. Since I can't do that, I have to work hard to stay young and engaged. Every person who can work and stay active has an obligation to do so. That's what I told Neil Cavuto one time when I was on Fox News. He was discussing the fact that the most recent estimates give the Social Security trust fund only until 2045 before it runs out of money. I weighed in, say-

ing, "Have everyone work as long as I have. That'll solve the problem." My solutions tend to be pretty straightforward.

Each of us is entitled to a second, third, and fourth act—as many
as possible. But it's necessary to stay physically and mentally fit to
keep yourself in the game. We are the only ones who can put limits on ourselves.

Several years ago, a journalist suggested I step aside and let
someone else have a turn. "You have a mistaken view of opportunity in America," I responded. "You see America as a feeding trough.
Someone needs to step aside to let someone else have a go at it.
The feeding trough in America is endless. Everyone can step up. All
you have to do is work hard and take advantage of the opportunities you're given."

I thank the Lord for letting me hang around as long as I have.
Every day is thrilling for me. I have had unusual success in predicting industry trends over the years, and I'm confident that many of
the things I have discussed and predicted in this book will become
a reality. These next few years are going to be particularly interesting—and critical for the world. I can't wait to see how it plays out.
One thing's for sure, I won't be on the sidelines. I'll be in the middle of the action. That's the only place for me.

Acknowledgments

THIS BOOK WAS a team effort, and my team came through for me, particularly everyone at BP Capital. Sally Geymüller, Gena Aduddell, Denise Delile, Susan Pepin, Bretta Price, and Monica Long juggled my schedule and managed to eke out the extra minutes, hours, and even days required to help me get the job done.

Andrew Littlefair read and reread every detail on natural gas, including the fine print on Clean Energy Fuels. Mike Reed did the same on our big-wind project. Oil and gas, energy, and equities—those topics were vetted by my ICM guys: Alex Szewczyk, Brian Bradshaw, David Meaney, and Michael Ross. Ron Bassett, Mike Boswell, Dick Grant, and Bobby Stillwell each took the time to review and make more accurate my recollection of events that chart the course of my career at Mesa and at BP Capital. My archivist, Judith Segura, did her usual top-notch job ensuring historical accuracy.

Jay Rosser deserves credit for bringing together all the pieces of the puzzle and has worked with me every step of the way. He'll continue to pitch in long after we go to press: scheduling interviews, setting up speeches, and handling the press.

I couldn't have been better served by my literary lineup. My wordsmiths—Mark Seal and Eric O'Keefe—helped turn one man's story into what they keep trying to convince me is a great read. I owe a debt of gratitude to Jan Miller at Dupree Miller & Associates for taking this project to the best possible publishing partner: Rick Horgan and Crown Business.

Finally, Madeleine, I want to thank you not only for putting up with the many inconveniences surrounding this lengthy project but also for your encouragement, inspiration, and love.

Index

Holder, Michael, 177, 178–80, 181, 182, 183
Hoopman, Harold "Hoop," 29
Horse Hollow wind farm, 240, 241
horse slaughter, 188–89
hostile takeovers, 28–29
Hotchkiss, Harley, 143
Hubbert, Marion King, 128
Hugoton Field, 14, 193
Hugoton Production Company, 14–17, 25, 26, 43, 62
Hull, T. G., 9, 172
hunches, Pickens view about, 75
Hurricane Katrina, 161, 186–88
hydrocarbon era, 245
hydroelectric power, 238

Iba, Henry, 173
Icahn, Carl, 41
India, 135, 139, 159
information, importance of, 64, 69, 75, 105, 106, 109, 124–25, 231
instincts, 83
interoffice relationships, 123
interstate highway system, 239
inventory, Pickens learns about, 20
involvement, importance of, 212
Iran, 19, 134, 136, 137–38, 159, 208
Iraq, 108, 136, 138, 156–57, 237

Jackson Dome (Mississippi), 144
Japan, nuclear energy in, 243
jobs, 133, 151, 233, 241

Karow, Marty, 172
Kashagan field (Caspian Sea), 134
Kelly, Dee, 54
kids at risk, Pickens gifts to, 165
Koch, Ed, 35
Koch Industries, 119
Kultgen, Bob, 59, 66, 82
Kuwait, oil in, 132, 135, 136–37

Larson, Mike, 82, 85, 93
Larson, Ron, 82, 85
lawn-mowing story, 43–44
Lay, Kenneth, 197
Lazard Frères investment firm, 39
leaders/leadership
  and alternative energy, 152
  availability to employees of, 125
  as coaches, 114–15
  decision-making of, 102
  and energy dependence, 3–4, 139
  and focus on future, 125
  function of, 115
  importance of, 115–16
  lack/failure of U.S., 3–4, 150, 228
  and listening, 124, 125
  and mistakes, 125
  and national energy plan, 236, 239, 241, 244, 245–46
  at OSU, 176, 183, 184
  and philanthropy, 166, 169, 176, 183
  of Reagan, 235–36
  as role models, 116
  and teamwork, 126

Lee, Jimmy, 21, 28, 33
Lee, John Ridings, 182
Leggett, Jeremy, 129
Lehman Brothers, 45
Lewis, Drew, 41–42
Liedtke, Bill, 204
Liedtke, Hugh, 204
life-insurance program, 182–83
"limit up," 110
limited partnerships, 64
Lindner, Carl, 41
liquefied natural gas (LNG), 203, 206, 208
listening, importance of, 65, 80, 121, 124, 125
Little, Jack, 81
Littlefair, Andrew, 50, 166, 191, 192, 198, 199, 200, 201, 202, 204, 207
Lonesome Dove (miniseries), 215–16
long-term investing, 76–77, 106
losing, 75, 77–78, 83–84
Louisiana, natural gas use in, 199
Louisiana State University, 187
loyalty, 116
luck, Pickens view about, 60

M. D. Anderson Cancer Center, 184
McClendon, Aubrey, 241
McKinney, Hondo, 59
McMurtry, Larry, 215
McShane, John, 70–71, 72–73, 77, 78, 86
Madden, Wales, 14, 15, 16, 17, 20
management fees, 85–86, 99
management philosophy, of Pickens, 114–26
Manhattan Project, 245
Marathon Oil, 29
Marcstone Capital, 100
Marvin Nichols Reservoir (Texas), 219–20
Matsuura, Koichiro, 213
Mauro, Garry, 196
Meaney, David, 89, 116–17
media, 18, 30, 111–12, 169, 189, 195. *See also specific reporter or organization*
Meinzer, Wyman, 218
Mellon family, 34
mergers and acquisitions, 7–8, 18, 19. *See also specific deal*
Merrill Lynch, 23
Mesa Environmental, 197–204
Mesa GEM (gas engine management) Kit, 197–98
Mesa Limited Partnership Preference stock, 43
Mesa Petroleum
  acquisition strategy of, 25–26
  Brumley as CEO of, 55
  Canadian operations of, 22
  and Cities Service deal, 26–31
  Clean Energy Fuels compared with, 208–9
  commodities trading at, 50–51, 60, 62, 63, 64, 65, 203
  corporate structure of, 42
  early investors in, 13
  employees stock ownership in, 123
  formation of, 13